Elements of Literature

First Course

S0-CFG-951

Language Handbook Worksheets

Additional Practice in Grammar, Usage, and Mechanics

*Correlated to Rules in the Language Handbook
in the Student Edition*

HOLT, RINEHART AND WINSTON

A Harcourt Education Company

Orlando • **Austin** • New York • San Diego • Toronto • London

Staff Credits

Associate Director: Mescal Evler

Manager of Editorial Operations: Robert R. Hoyt

Managing Editor: Bill Wahlgren

Project Editor: Katie Vignery

Component Editors: Marcia Kelley, Karen H. Kolar, James Hynes

Editorial Staff: *Associate Editors,* Kathryn Rogers, Christopher LeCluyse; *Assistant Managing Editor,* Mandy Beard; *Copyediting Supervisor,* Michael Neibergall; *Senior Copyeditor,* Mary Malone; *Copyeditors,* Joel Bourgeois, Jeffrey T. Holt, Jane Kominek, Désirée Reid, Suzi A. Hunn; *Editorial Coordinators,* Marie H. Price, Robert Littlefield, Mark Holland, Jill Chertudi, Tracy DeMont, Marcus Johnson; *Support Staff,* Pat Stover, Matthew Villalobos; *Word Processors,* Ruth Hooker, Margaret Sanchez, Kelly Keeley, Elizabeth Butler

Permissions: Tamara A. Blanken, Ann B. Farrar

Design: *Art Director, Book Design,* Richard Metzger; *Design Manager, Book & Media Design,* Joe Melomo

Prepress Production: Beth Prevelige, Simira Davis, Sergio Durante

Manufacturing Coordinator: Michael Roche

Copyright © by Holt, Rinehart and Winston

All rights reserved. No part of this publication may be reproduced or transmitted in any form or by any means, electronic or mechanical, including photocopy, recording, or any information storage and retrieval system, without permission in writing from the publisher.

Teachers using ELEMENTS OF LITERATURE may photocopy blackline masters in complete pages in sufficient quantities for classroom use only and not for resale.

Printed in the United States of America

ISBN 0-03-073918-7

1 2 3 4 5 6 179 04 03

TABLE OF CONTENTS

LANGUAGE HANDBOOK 1
THE PARTS OF SPEECH

LANGUAGE HANDBOOK 2
AGREEMENT

LANGUAGE HANDBOOK 3
USING VERBS

Copyright © by Holt, Rinehart and Winston. All rights reserved.

LANGUAGE HANDBOOK 4
USING PRONOUNS

LANGUAGE HANDBOOK 5
USING MODIFIERS

LANGUAGE HANDBOOK 6
PHRASES

Copyright © by Holt, Rinehart and Winston. All rights reserved.

LANGUAGE HANDBOOK 7
CLAUSES

LANGUAGE HANDBOOK 8
SENTENCES

LANGUAGE HANDBOOK 9
COMPLEMENTS

Copyright © by Holt, Rinehart and Winston. All rights reserved.

LANGUAGE HANDBOOK 10
KINDS OF SENTENCES

LANGUAGE HANDBOOK 11
WRITING EFFECTIVE SENTENCES

LANGUAGE HANDBOOK 12
CAPITAL LETTERS

LANGUAGE HANDBOOK 13
PUNCTUATION

Copyright © by Holt, Rinehart and Winston. All rights reserved.

LANGUAGE HANDBOOK 14
PUNCTUATION

LANGUAGE HANDBOOK 15
PUNCTUATION

LANGUAGE HANDBOOK 16
SPELLING

LANGUAGE HANDBOOK 17
GLOSSARY OF USAGE

Copyright © by Holt, Rinehart and Winston. All rights reserved.

This booklet, *Language Handbook Worksheets,* contains practice and reinforcement copying masters that cover the material presented in the Language Handbook section of *Elements of Literature, First Course.* The rules cited in the head of each worksheet correspond directly to the grammar, usage, and mechanics rules and instruction covered in the Language Handbook. Tests at the end of each section can also be used as end-of-section reviews.

A separate *Answer Key* for the *Language Handbook Worksheets* provides answers or suggested responses to all items in this booklet.

Copyright © by Holt, Rinehart and Winston. All rights reserved.

LANGUAGE HANDBOOK **1** THE PARTS OF SPEECH

WORKSHEET 1 | Nouns (Rule 1 a)

EXERCISE A   On the lines provided, write five common nouns that name persons, five that name places, five that name things, and five that name ideas. Read the example of each type of noun before you write.

	Persons	*Places*	*Things*	*Ideas*
EXAMPLE 1.	child	city	piñata	truth
1.				
2.				
3.				
4.				
5.				

EXERCISE B   Fill in the blanks in the following sentences with appropriate nouns. Do not use any noun more than once.

EXAMPLE 1. Sachi wore a beautiful ___kimono___ to the ___celebration___.

1. The _____ tastes even better than the _____.

2. The group's new _____ has lots of _____.

3. My _____ is painted red and green.

4. Radha likes _____ better than _____.

5. Geoffrey stood on a _____ to hang the _____.

6. _____ and _____ are much bigger than _____.

7. _____ and _____ are both in my math class.

8. We used the _____ while the _____ was broken.

9. Marta bought a silver _____ instead of a _____.

10. She made _____ with her new _____.

Copyright © by Holt, Rinehart and Winston. All rights reserved.

Continued ☞

LANGUAGE HANDBOOK **1** **WORKSHEET 1** *(continued)*

EXERCISE C In each of the following sentences, underline all of the common nouns and circle the proper nouns.

EXAMPLE 1. For <u>weeks</u> the (Juarezes) had planned a <u>trip</u>.

1. One Saturday the family packed their minivan and drove to Catawba Lake.

2. Because Highway 10 was uncrowded, the drive took only thirty minutes.

3. The water in the lake was just the right temperature.

4. The swimming area has a pier and a raft with a diving board.

5. Adela and her brother, Enrique, dived into the lake and enjoyed the water for about an hour.

6. You can imagine their disappointment when clouds rolled in.

7. The sky turned dark, and a thunderstorm began.

8. As Adela and Enrique quickly swam to shore, the first raindrops fell.

9. Just as the family reached their minivan, the rain began coming down harder.

10. They drove to The Angler, a nearby restaurant, and enjoyed a pizza.

EXERCISE D For each of the following sentences, underline each compound or collective noun. Then, above compound nouns, write *CP*. Above collective nouns, write *CL*.

          CL   *CP*

EXAMPLE 1. An <u>army</u> of ants trooped to our table at <u>Davis Park</u>.

1. Who was elected sergeant-at-arms of your club?

2. Many purebred horses in this herd have long pedigrees.

3. The Russians bred wolfhounds for speed.

4. When will our class visit the bookmobile again?

5. Is Toni Morrison really coming to visit your school?

Copyright © by Holt, Rinehart and Winston. All rights reserved.

LANGUAGE
HANDBOOK **1** THE PARTS OF SPEECH

| WORKSHEET 2 | Pronouns (Rule 1 b)

EXERCISE A   Underline all of the pronouns in the following paragraphs.

> **EXAMPLE**   [1] Kam Shing, <u>who</u> is <u>my</u> best friend, and <u>I</u> had gathered the materials <u>that</u> <u>we</u> would need for <u>our</u> science project.

[1] Mother saw Kam Shing and me at the door and asked us where we were going. [2] I had on my hiking boots, and Kam Shing was carrying a knapsack on her back. [3] "You remember, Mom. We are going on a field trip," I reminded her. [4] "Our science teacher, Mrs. Echohawk, is going to show us how to build a tepee."

[5] "Oh, yes. That sounds like an interesting project," she replied. [6] "Be sure to stay with your classmates. [7] I don't want either of you getting lost."

[8] We told her we would be careful.

[9] Everyone in our science class had looked forward to our field trip to Osceola Woods Park. [10] When we arrived, we found a troop of Scouts in the clearing.

[11] "What are they doing here?" we wondered. [12] Mrs. Echohawk had reserved that space with the park ranger himself.

[13] "The clearing will be too crowded if they stay," I thought to myself.

[14] We decided to talk to the scoutmaster, but none of the Scouts could tell us where he was. [15] They were by themselves. [16] Several suggested that he must have gone for water. [17] Others thought he might be searching for a good trail. [18] One believed he was foraging for berries.

[19] Then someone said, "The scoutmaster is coming back." [20] We saw him bringing a large pail of water. [21] The Scouts all filled their canteens from it. [22] As soon as their canteens were filled, they were ready to leave. [23] The troop picked up their packs and hiked off. [24] At last we had the clearing entirely to ourselves. [25] Then Mrs. Echohawk showed us how to build a tepee.

Copyright © by Holt, Rinehart and Winston. All rights reserved.

Continued ☞

LANGUAGE HANDBOOK **1** **WORKSHEET 2** *(continued)*

EXERCISE B In the following paragraph, cross out each word or word group in italics and write a suitable pronoun above it.

> *She*
> **EXAMPLE** [1] Ginny Johnson is a remarkable student. ~~Ginny~~ plans to be
> a physicist.

[1] *Ginny* is the only student in our class who knows what career [2] *the student*
wants to have. The rest of [3] *the students* haven't decided yet. Ginny is already studying
algebra. [4] *Ginny* gets special tutoring from teachers in other subjects. Everyone in
[5] *Ginny's* family is remarkable. [6] *Ginny's* older brother is a champion wrestler and a
halfback on the high school football team. [7] *Ginny's older brother's* name is Percy, but
nobody calls [8] *Percy* that because [9] *Percy* doesn't like it. Everyone calls [10] *Percy*
"Perce." [11] *Ginny and Percy's* mother is a famous singer. [12] *Ginny and Percy's*
mother was performing when [13] *the mother* met [14] *Ginny and Percy's* father.
[15] *Ginny and Percy's* father is the state champion mah-jongg player. [16] *The father* is
teaching Ginny how to play mah-jongg. Perce already knows how to play the game.
[17] *Perce* and Ginny play almost every day. [18] *Perce and Ginny* also know how to play
bridge, but [19] *Perce and Ginny* prefer mah-jongg. I always enjoy visiting the Johnsons
because [20] *the Johnsons* are a very friendly and fascinating family.

Copyright © by Holt, Rinehart and Winston. All rights reserved.

LANGUAGE HANDBOOK 1 · THE PARTS OF SPEECH

WORKSHEET 3 | Adjectives (Rule 1 c)

EXERCISE A   Underline all the adjectives in the following sentences, and draw an arrow from each adjective to the word it modifies. Do not underline the articles *a, an,* and *the.*

> EXAMPLE **1.** Despite the <u>terrible</u> heat, everyone had a <u>good</u>, <u>relaxing</u> time.

1. A hot, dry wind blew over the parched Midwestern town of Sallisaw, Oklahoma.

2. Some citizens believed that the weather pattern of El Niño caused the hot weather.

3. The uncomfortable people sought out the shadiest, coolest spots.

4. The thunderheads on the horizon were huge and black.

5. Panting dogs hid under the thickest bushes.

6. Vendors sold cold drinks to thirsty children.

7. Some people in the hot town stayed in their cool and comfortable homes.

8. The long, hot day drew to a close in a fiery sunset.

9. Thunder rolled from the storm clouds, and a delightful cool wind stirred the dusty trees along the main street of the town.

10. Soon a heavy rainstorm brought an end to the hot weather.

EXERCISE B   Underline each adjective in the following sentences. Do not underline the articles *a, an,* and *the.* Then, draw an arrow from each adjective to the word it modifies.

> EXAMPLE **1.** Mr. Pekarcik, our <u>science</u> teacher, showed us an <u>interesting</u> film.

1. Natural latex, which comes from trees in dense tropical forests, is an important and useful substance.

2. There were few ways to use latex in everyday living until the nineteenth century.

3. Latex was not even given the ordinary name of rubber until a famous scientist discovered that it could rub out pencil marks.

4. The first practical use of the substance was as an eraser.

5. It was also used to make waterproof coats.

6. These early coats became sticky in hot weather and brittle in cold weather.

7. An inventor, Charles Goodyear, found ways to make rubber less changeable.

8. His discoveries led to many new uses of the substance.

9. For example, rubber is used for elastic bands, athletic shoes, and all kinds of tires.

10. The mass production of synthetic rubber began in 1942, and today more products are made from this synthetic material than from natural rubber.

Copyright © by Holt, Rinehart and Winston. All rights reserved.

LANGUAGE HANDBOOK **1** THE PARTS OF SPEECH

WORKSHEET 4 | Verbs (Rules 1 d, g)

EXERCISE A   Underline the verb in each of the following sentences.

> **EXAMPLE 1.** Toni <u>played</u> the bass guitar.

1. Rosamunda accompanied her on rhythm guitar.
2. They formed a musical group with two other friends.
3. They had many rehearsals and practice sessions.
4. After several months of practice, the group sounded very professional.
5. Suddenly the lead vocalist, Toshi, moved to another city.
6. Akela took Toshi's place.
7. Everyone in the group liked her style of singing.
8. Chee became the manager for the quartet.
9. They performed for an enthusiastic audience at the summer concert.
10. This performance marked the beginning of a successful career for the band.

EXERCISE B   Underline the main verbs and circle the helping verbs in the following paragraph.

> **EXAMPLE** [1] (Have) you ever <u>studied</u> the geography of France?

[1] Natural barriers have always separated France from neighboring countries. [2] On the north, west, and south, France is protected by the sea. [3] The Pyrenees chain forms the rest of France's southern border. [4] The Alps rise in the southeast. [5] Mont Blanc, Europe's highest point, is located in the French Alps. [6] In the east are the Vosges Mountains. [7] The main danger of invasion always has lain to the northeast. [8] There, France and Germany meet along the banks of the Rhine River. [9] For approximately one hundred miles, the Rhine River serves as France's eastern border. [10] Between France and Belgium, the land boundary crosses flat, open country.

Copyright © by Holt, Rinehart and Winston. All rights reserved.

LANGUAGE HANDBOOK 1 **THE PARTS OF SPEECH**

| **WORSHEET 5** | Action Verbs and Linking Verbs (Rules 1 e, f)

EXERCISE A The verb in each of the following sentences is italicized. On the line provided, write *A* if the verb is an action verb or *L* if it is a linking verb.

EXAMPLE ___L___ 1. "The Hummingbird King" *is* a popular folk tale.

_____ 1. The seventh-graders at our school *produced* a play last year.

_____ 2. The students *wrote* the entertaining play themselves.

_____ 3. They *based* the play on the Mayan folk tale "The Hummingbird King."

_____ 4. Mr. Nuñez, our English teacher, *became* the director of the play.

_____ 5. The play *portrayed* the origin of the <u>quetzal</u>, a colorful bird.

_____ 6. All the seventh-graders in the play *were* outstanding.

_____ 7. The production of the play *went* smoothly, in spite of a few setbacks.

_____ 8. The audience *enjoyed* the play immensely.

_____ 9. They *applauded* with enthusiasm at the end.

_____ 10. Mr. Nuñez and the seventh-graders *seemed* pleased with their dramatic version of the Mayan folk tale.

EXERCISE B Underline the verb, including any helping verbs, in each of the following sentences. On the line provided, write *A* if the verb is an action verb; write *L* if it is a linking verb.

EXAMPLE ___A___ 1. We <u>are listening</u> to the music of Scott Joplin.

_____ 1. Sharal's father served bagels for breakfast.

_____ 2. Joseph Bruchac has recorded many Iroquois folk tales.

_____ 3. Have you read any of Bruchac's stories?

_____ 4. The key will be left in the glove compartment.

_____ 5. The giant panda of China remains an endangered species.

_____ 6. Our best friends may sometimes be our harshest critics.

_____ 7. She probably would have walked home along the river.

_____ 8. The quarterback felt refreshed after a short rest.

_____ 9. The new school could not possibly be ready in six months.

_____ 10. Benjamin Banneker was a famous American astronomer.

Copyright © by Holt, Rinehart and Winston. All rights reserved.

WORKSHEET 6 | Adverbs (Rule 1 h)

EXERCISE A Circle each adverb in the following sentences, and draw an arrow from the adverb to the word it modifies.

EXAMPLE 1. (Often) at our house we start do-it-yourself projects.

1. Dan and I recently decided on a special project.
2. We very cautiously shortened the legs of an old dresser.
3. Next, we placed a piece of plywood on top of the dresser.
4. Carefully, Dan nailed the plywood to the top of the dresser.
5. We proudly showed our parents this new desk.
6. They then suggested a new coat of paint.
7. I looked around for a totally clean brush.
8. Dan had stored a can of paint somewhere.
9. Finally, we found the paint in the garage.
10. Dan and I soon had the desk painted.

EXERCISE B In the following paragraph, fill in the blanks with appropriate adverbs. Try to vary your choice of adverbs.

EXAMPLE Every Thursday afternoon, Neve goes [1] __directly__ from school to her piano lesson.

Neve arrives [1] _____ at her piano teacher's house. Her piano teacher, Mrs.

Katzenberg, [2] _____ delays Neve's lesson by keeping another pupil overtime.

Neve [3] _____ sits for a long time, waiting. Arsenio, the student whose lesson is

before Neve's, plays [4] _____. Neve never plays [5] _____, but she

does not always play [6] _____, either. When Arsenio [7] _____

finishes, Mrs. Katzenberg [8] _____ comes out to say hello. Neve likes to

play the piano but does not like to practice. She knows, however, that to play

[9] _____, she has to practice [10] _____.

Copyright © by Holt, Rinehart and Winston. All rights reserved.

LANGUAGE HANDBOOK 1 THE PARTS OF SPEECH

WORKSHEET 7 **Identifying Adjectives and Adverbs (Rules 1 c, h)**

EXERCISE A Identify the italicized modifiers in the following sentences. In the space above each modifier, write *ADJ* if it is an adjective or *ADV* if it is an adverb.

                                        ADJ   ADV

        EXAMPLE 1. I watched the *early* show, but I did not go to bed *early*.

1. The plane circled the *vacant* field and *slowly* came in for a *smooth* landing.

2. You should not drive too *fast;* however, a *slow* driver can be dangerous, too.

3. Mira has been *faithfully* practicing the cello *lately*.

4. Luisa *politely* interrupted Arny's *leisurely* account of his *recent* trip.

5. Miss Remington *certainly* does work *hard*.

6. Pandas have *hardly ever* been born in captivity.

7. The *green* bus *nearly* had a *slight* accident yesterday.

8. Tom walked toward the *red* squirrel *quickly,* and the squirrel ran *away*.

9. Mr. Acoli *first* said to make up the test, but his *second* idea was to write a report.

10. "You will go *far,* young man," Dr. Hounsou *often* assured me.

EXERCISE B In the following paragraphs, underline all the adjectives and circle all the adverbs. Do not underline the articles *a, an,* and *the*.

        EXAMPLE [1] Many years (ago,) the New York drama critics (proudly) gave
                           Lorraine Hansberry their (highly) respected award for the
                           best American play of the new theater season.

    [1] At that time, Lorraine Hansberry was the youngest American playwright, the first woman, and the first African American to receive the honor. [2] Her much celebrated play was *A Raisin in the Sun*.

    [3] Hansberry deeply believed that all people have within them the ability somehow to change the universe dramatically. [4] She clearly understood the vast power of human potential when it has been nurtured. [5] Because she saw the incredible beauty of every person, she wisely knew that it is an enormous error to waste life. [6] She recognized that each person has a dream. [7] If the dream dies, then a very important part of life surely dies. [8] No good dream should be allowed to shrivel slowly like "a raisin in the sun."

    [9] *A Raisin in the Sun* was also produced on Broadway as a musical. [10] Called *Raisin,* it incorporates the music and dances of African peoples.

Copyright © by Holt, Rinehart and Winston. All rights reserved.

LANGUAGE HANDBOOK 1 THE PARTS OF SPEECH

WORKSHEET 8 **Prepositions (Rule 1 i)**

EXERCISE A   Complete the following sentences by writing appropriate prepositions in the blanks. Try to use as many different prepositions as possible.

EXAMPLE **1.** __*At*__ noon Joaquin and I were still many miles __*from*__ our home in Estancia.

1. Joaquin and I rode our bicycles _____ the bridge and _____ the trail.

2. _____ an hour, we had traveled ten miles.

3. _____ this rate, we would reach Estancia _____ evening.

4. There was a good wind _____ us.

5. Joaquin rode _____ some broken glass.

6. _____ fifteen minutes, his front tire went flat.

7. Joaquin repaired the tire _____ a short time.

8. _____ that we rested.

9. Then, we continued riding _____ our destination.

10. Tired and hungry, we arrived home shortly _____ sunset.

EXERCISE B   Underline each prepositional phrase in the paragraph below. Circle each object of a preposition.

EXAMPLE [1] The turtle is regarded <u>as an important (animal)</u> <u>in the (cultures)</u> <u>of many (American Indians.)</u>

[1] Some of the American Indian nations that show respect for the turtle are the Hopi,

Snake, and Iroquois. [2] These peoples show their respect in ceremonial dances. [3] The

dancers wear turtle-shell rattles at their knees and belts of bells around their waists.

[4] Each dancer carries a gourd rattle in the right hand. [5] During the turtle dance, the

performers imitate the movements of the turtle.

Copyright © by Holt, Rinehart and Winston. All rights reserved.

LANGUAGE HANDBOOK **1** THE PARTS OF SPEECH

WORKSHEET 9 Conjunctions and Interjections (Rules 1 j, k)

EXERCISE A   The following sentences contain conjunctions and interjections. Underline each conjunction, and circle each interjection. Remember to underline both parts of the correlative conjunctions that you find.

EXAMPLE   **1.** (Wow!) The dress <u>and</u> scarf look beautiful together.

1. Brrr! This is such a cold and rainy day.

2. I am wearing warm clothes, but I am still very cold.

3. Neither Maya nor Anika has read "The No-Guitar Blues" by Gary Soto.

4. Have you read his novels *Taking Sides* and *Pacific Crossing*?

5. Gee, this is a really easy assignment!

6. Well, I can't help you with the concession stand, but Abasi may be able to help you.

7. Oh well, we can't expect our team to win every game.

8. Neither Antoine nor Derek was well enough to play in the game.

9. Both Sarah and Anetta play not only the saxophone but also the cello.

10. Goodness! Do you think that either Sarah or Anetta would like to join our band?

EXERCISE B   In each of the following sentences, insert the conjunction *and, but,* or *or,* depending on which makes the most sense.

EXAMPLE   **1.** The pond was frozen, ___*and*___ we decided to go ice-skating.

1. Pat lives next door to me, _____ we never walk to school together.

2. Our house is painted yellow, _____ the shutters are painted white.

3. Ann Boston is the class president, _____ she is also the yearbook editor.

4. You can rake the lawn, _____ you can do the dishes.

5. Pearl must be sick, _____ she would be in school today.

6. The oak was struck by lightning, _____ it is still alive.

7. Rosalie worked in a lumberyard, _____ Mario delivered newspapers.

8. I washed the car on Saturday, _____ today I am going on a picnic.

9. Paul studied for three hours, _____ he forgot to memorize the poem.

10. Bart promised to pay me back, _____ he never did.

Copyright © by Holt, Rinehart and Winston. All rights reserved.

LANGUAGE HANDBOOK **1** **THE PARTS OF SPEECH**

WORSHEET 10 **Which Part of Speech? (Rules 1 a–d, h–j)**

EXERCISE A   On the line provided, identify the part of speech of each italicized word in the following sentences. Use the abbreviations *N* for noun, *PRON* for pronoun, *V* for verb, *ADJ* for adjective, *ADV* for adverb, *PREP* for preposition, *CONJ* for conjunction, or *INTERJ* for interjection.

EXAMPLES ____*V*____ **1.** The rain may *last* all afternoon.

____*ADJ*____ **2.** She was the *last* person in line.

_____ **1.** *Wow!* I will be in the school *play,* The Panda's Wish.

_____ **2.** The *swift* current here is *dangerously* strong.

_____ **3.** Are you coming *over* tonight to *play* computer games?

_____ **4.** Can *you reverse* the order of the players?

_____ **5.** We looked *for* Alicia at the library, *for* we knew she was there.

EXERCISE B   The following paragraph contains twenty-five numbered, italicized words. Identify the part of speech of each italicized word by writing, on the line provided, one of the following abbreviations: *N* for noun, *PRON* for pronoun, *V* for verb, *ADJ* for adjective, *ADV* for adverb, *PREP* for preposition, *CONJ* for conjunction, or *INTERJ* for interjection.

EXAMPLE Polar bears live in cold, [1] *northern* ____*ADJ*____ regions.

The [1] *large,* _____ white bears live mainly in coastal [2] *arctic* _____

[3] *regions.* _____ Armed with a [4] *very* _____ sharp sense [5] *of* _____

smell, the bears [6] *are* _____ excellent hunters. Amazingly, they can [7] *smell*

_____ food as far as ten miles away! [8] *They* _____ are also excellent

[9] *swimmers* _____ in [10] *icy* _____ waters. They [11] *often* _____

swim up to seals floating on ice floes [12] *and* _____ pounce on [13] *their*

_____ unsuspecting prey. Polar bears [14] *rarely* _____ kill people, [15] *but*

_____ don't try to outrun a bear [16] *on* _____ land. [17] *Yikes!* _____

They can run up to thirty-five miles an hour in [18] *short* _____ spurts! When polar

bears are born, they are [19] *only* _____ ten inches long. [20] *Who* _____

would believe the tiny [21] *creatures* _____ can grow [22] *into* _____ fearsome

adults weighing over one thousand pounds? Today, [23] *these* _____ beautiful

animals [24] *are* _____ protected from hunters [25] *by* _____ law.

Copyright © by Holt, Rinehart and Winston. All rights reserved.

Elements of Literature

LANGUAGE HANDBOOK **1** THE PARTS OF SPEECH

WORKSHEET 11 Test (Rules 1 a–k)

EXERCISE A   The following paragraph contains twenty numbered, italicized words or phrases. Identify the part of speech of each italicized word by writing, on the line provided, one of the following abbreviations: *N* for noun, *PRON* for pronoun, *V* for verb, *ADJ* for adjective, *ADV* for adverb, *PREP* for preposition, *CONJ* for conjunction, or *INTERJ* for interjection.

> **EXAMPLES** [1] *In* ___PREP___ June the Osaka [2] *family* ____N____
>
> went on vacation to [3] *New York City.* ____N____

The Osakas spent [1] *three* _____ days sightseeing in New York City. [2] *On*

_____ the first day, [3] *they* _____ took a tour bus to see [4] *some* _____

of the [5] *famous* _____ parts of the city. The bus took them to Wall Street,

Chinatown, Greenwich Village, [6] *and* _____ many other [7] *incredibly* _____

fascinating places. The next day, the Osakas [8] *decided* _____ to go to the [9] *top*

_____ of the Empire State Building. [10] *Oh,* _____ the view was spectacular!

The sky was [11] *unusually* _____ clear; they [12] *could* _____ see as far as

Connecticut! That evening, they ate at a quaint restaurant [13] *that* _____ serves

delicious [14] *Chinese* _____ food. [15] *Afterward,* _____ they went to Radio

City Music Hall, where an [16] *elaborate* _____ stage show entertained them. On

their third day of sightseeing, the Osakas visited the [17] *Statue of Liberty.* _____

This historical landmark greatly [18] *impressed* _____ every member of the Osaka

family. The [19] *next* _____ day, as the Osakas prepared to go home, they agreed

that they would come [20] *back* _____ to New York City for their next vacation.

EXERCISE B   Identify the part of speech of the italicized word or words in each of the following sentences. Use the abbreviations *N* for noun, *PRON* for pronoun, *V* for verb, *ADJ* for adjective, *ADV* for adverb, *PREP* for preposition, *CONJ* for conjunction, or *INTERJ* for interjection. Write the abbreviations on the lines provided.

> **EXAMPLE** ___ADJ___ **1.** "Yeh-Shen" is the *Chinese* version of the story "Cinderella."

_____ **1.** This book is for you *and* Katya.

_____ **2.** The horse stumbled on the first *step* and refused to budge.

Copyright © by Holt, Rinehart and Winston. All rights reserved.

Continued ☞

_____ **3.** Winnie ate a *leisurely* breakfast and sauntered off to school.

_____ **4.** Do you *like* honey or lemon in your herbal tea?

_____ **5.** Silence fell in the room *like* a weight.

_____ **6.** Carmen has the *will* to succeed.

_____ **7.** Work *fast,* or you will never finish in time.

_____ **8.** Geraldo ran a *fast* first kilometer in the race.

_____ **9.** Siobhan gave the orchestra conductor a *friendly* smile.

_____ **10.** We all had a good *swim* at the lake.

_____ **11.** Do you ever *swim* at Lake Mancuso?

_____ **12.** Cortez Street was *nearly* deserted.

_____ **13.** *Beside* the computer desk was a tall brass lamp.

_____ **14.** The students sat *quietly,* reading the German folk tale "Aschenputtel."

_____ **15.** I sleep on a *down* pillow at my grandmother's house.

_____ **16.** Look *down* the mountain, and tell me what you see.

_____ **17.** The runner fell *down* at the finish of the race.

_____ **18.** They get their water from a *well.*

_____ **19.** *Well,* it's nice to see you.

_____ **20.** The camera belongs to *either* Ernesto *or* Myron.

_____ **21.** As she waited impatiently, she looked at her *watch.*

_____ **22.** Will you please *watch* the soup so that it doesn't boil?

_____ **23.** *Each* contestant must sign up before the race.

_____ **24.** *Each* has competed in previous races.

_____ **25.** *What* do you want to take with you?

Copyright © by Holt, Rinehart and Winston. All rights reserved.

Copyright © by Holt, Rinehart and Winston. All rights reserved.

LANGUAGE HANDBOOK 2 AGREEMENT

WORKSHEET 1 **Agreement of Subject and Verb (Rule 2 a)**

EXERCISE A Identify the number (singular or plural) of each word below. On the line provided, write *S* for singular or *P* for plural.

EXAMPLE __*S*__ **1.** pizza

_____ **1.** birds		_____ **11.** women	
_____ **2.** clock		_____ **12.** kayak	
_____ **3.** princess		_____ **13.** he	
_____ **4.** bicycle		_____ **14.** children	
_____ **5.** they		_____ **15.** oxen	
_____ **6.** tacos		_____ **16.** ribbon	
_____ **7.** teeth		_____ **17.** lice	
_____ **8.** cloud		_____ **18.** waltzes	
_____ **9.** scarves		_____ **19.** mouse	
_____ **10.** kimonos		_____ **20.** leaves	

EXERCISE B In the following sentences, circle the singular nouns and underline the plural nouns.

EXAMPLE **1.** Some people carry a four-leaf clover or other charm for good luck.

1. One type of superstition is a belief that a certain action will cause a second action that is totally unrelated.

2. Superstitions have existed in all civilizations and in all times.

3. Although superstitions are often a result of ignorance, even educated people hold superstitions.

4. Many superstitions have been passed from generation to generation.

5. If your parents knocked on wood for good luck, you might do so, too.

6. My friend Roseanne used to believe that opening an umbrella in the house is unlucky.

7. Some people fear that a black cat crossing in front of them will bring them bad luck.

8. Others are confident that finding a horseshoe will bring them good luck.

9. Would you walk under a ladder, or do you think doing so might bring you bad luck?

10. A common belief among my friends is that to break a mirror means seven years of bad luck.

LANGUAGE HANDBOOK **2** **AGREEMENT**

| WORSHEET 2 | **Agreement of Subject and Verb (Rule 2 b)**

EXERCISE A   In each of the following sentences, underline the verb in parentheses that agrees in number with the subject.

> **EXAMPLE 1.** The Murphys (*lives, live*) in Washington, D.C.

1. They (*enjoys, enjoy*) traveling by train.

2. The *Metroliners* (*connect, connects*) New York and Washington, D.C.

3. The Murphys (*pays, pay*) for their tickets at Union Station.

4. Before the train (*leaves, leave*), the conductor shouts, "All aboard!"

5. Other trains (*is passing, are passing*) their train at high speeds.

6. Brian stays awake, but his sister, Caroline, (*falls, fall*) asleep.

7. The conductors (*is asking, are asking*) for tickets.

8. Brian (*shake, shakes*) his sleeping sister to wake her.

9. "We (*has passed, have passed*) Baltimore," he tells her.

10. "Wake me when the train (*reach, reaches*) New York," she replies.

EXERCISE B   On the line provided, rewrite each of the following sentences by changing the number of its subject and verb. Make singular subjects and verbs plural; make plural subjects and verbs singular.

> **EXAMPLE 1.** Clouds cover the sky along the horizon.
> <u>A cloud covers the sky along the horizon.</u>

1. The riderless horse was galloping wildly across the pampas.

_____

2. The New England coastal city closes the beaches in September.

_____

3. They like to daydream about traveling to faraway places, such as Hong Kong, Pago Pago, and Madagascar.

_____

4. Last summer I was at the beach almost every day.

_____

5. The elm trees have been growing here for a century.

_____

Copyright © by Holt, Rinehart and Winston. All rights reserved.

Elements of Literature

LANGUAGE HANDBOOK **2** **AGREEMENT**

WORKSHEET 3 **Agreement of Subject and Verb (Rule 2 c)**

EXERCISE A In each of the following sentences, one or more prepositional phrases separate the subject from the verb. Cross out each prepositional phrase. Then, underline the verb in parentheses that agrees in number with the subject.

EXAMPLE 1. Dozens ~~of pigeons~~ ~~from the pen~~ ~~on the roof~~ (*flies, fly*) in circles.

1. One person among the new members (*objects, object*) to the proposal.

2. The cows in the herd (*turns, turn*) their backs to the storm.

3. The date of our production of *Purlie Victorious* (*has, have*) not yet been set.

4. A portion of the money rightfully (*belongs, belong*) to Laura.

5. This new book about the nations of Africa (*includes, include*) up-to-date maps.

EXERCISE B In each of the following sentences, underline the correct verb in parentheses.

EXAMPLE 1. Movies such as *Independence Day* and *Star Trek: Generations* (*suggests, suggest*) that there is life on other planets.

1. Scientists at a leading American university (*has, have*) collected jokes about life on other planets.

2. In their opinion, jokes about outer space (*reveal, reveals*) people's hidden fears of the unknown.

3. Perhaps a civilization on one of the distant planets (*has, have*) grown more powerful than Earth's.

4. If invaders from one of these older and wiser civilizations (*come, comes*) to Earth, will earthlings know how to respond to them?

5. Questions of this kind apparently (*worry, worries*) some people.

6. According to the scientists, jokes about space invaders (*calm, calms*) people's inner fears.

7. Often, the invaders in these jokes (*turn, turns*) out to be not so intelligent after all.

8. One short story about two Martians (*is, are*) especially amusing.

9. The creatures from Mars walk up to a parked car and (*order, orders*) it to take them to its leader. The car says nothing.

10. Finally, one Martian, after repeated threats, (*kick, kicks*) the car and breaks its headlights. "Shame on you!" says the other Martian. "You broke its glasses!"

Copyright © by Holt, Rinehart and Winston. All rights reserved.

Elements of Literature

WORKSHEET 4	**Agreement of Subject and Verb (Rules 2 b–f)**

EXERCISE A   In each of the following sentences, draw one line under the subject and two lines under the verb form in parentheses that agrees in number with the subject.

EXAMPLE **1.** <u>One</u> of my brothers (*work, <u>works</u>*) in Alaska.

1. Both of these games (*interests, interest*) my father.

2. Neither of the bulls (*was, were*) a prize winner at the state fair.

3. Either of your suggestions for the meeting (*suit, suits*) me.

4. Everyone from the schools (*is, are*) going to the Juneteenth celebration.

5. Most of the cars (*needs, need*) a wash after a week of rain.

6. Few, however, (*stay, stays*) in their seats for very long.

7. All of the food in the Indian restaurant's buffet (*look, looks*) delicious.

8. Each of these young people (*has, have*) visited the mission at San Miguel.

9. Several of the English poets (*is, are*) buried in Westminster Abbey.

10. Anyone with a love of mystery stories (*enjoy, enjoys*) Agatha Christie's books.

EXERCISE B   In most of the following sentences, the verbs do not agree with their subjects. Cross out each incorrect verb, and write the correct form on the line provided. If the verb is already correct, write *C*.

EXAMPLE ___*is*___ **1.** One of my friends ~~are~~ writing a report on Harriet Tubman.

_____ **1.** Neither of the two researchers were aware of the problem.

_____ **2.** Everyone in the room were talking at once.

_____ **3.** Every fall the apples from this one tree fills several baskets.

_____ **4.** A recent story in the newspapers tells of a prize cabbage weighing nineteen kilograms.

_____ **5.** Several members of my class has been absent this week.

_____ **6.** Two bales of wastepaper was lying in the middle of the road.

_____ **7.** A pound of feathers weigh as much as a pound of gold.

_____ **8.** Some of these names are derived from American Indian languages.

_____ **9.** One of these books describe the operation of the Underground Railroad.

_____ **10.** A box of old coins were buried at the foot of a large oak tree.

Copyright © by Holt, Rinehart and Winston. All rights reserved.

Elements of Literature

WORKSHEET 5 | Agreement of Subject and Verb (Rules 2 g, h, k)

EXERCISE A For each of the following sentences, underline the verb that agrees with the subject.

> **EXAMPLE 1.** Five nickels or one quarter (*equals*, *equal*) twenty-five cents.

1. Jeans, cowboy boots, a tuxedo coat, a tie, and a dress shirt (*makes up*, *make up*) what is known as a Texas tuxedo.

2. A fox or some raccoons (*has*, *have*) created quite a mess out in the stables.

3. Neither rain nor snow nor sleet nor unfriendly dogs (*stops*, *stop*) the delivery of mail.

4. Then as now, business interests and public demand (*fuels*, *fuel*) exploration of the natural world.

5. Among artists and decorators, green and blue (*is*, *are*) known as "cool" colors.

6. As far as I know, neither Florida nor the other southern states (*has*, *have*) wild lilies of the valley.

7. The birds and butterflies of South America surely (*is*, *are*) among the most colorful in the world.

8. Either her parents or Wendy (*watches*, *watch*) every one of Jesse's games.

9. Haiti and the Dominican Republic (*occupies*, *occupy*) the same island—Hispaniola.

10. A few flowers or a shrub (*brightens*, *brighten*) any yard.

EXERCISE B Underline the subject of each of the following sentences. Then, on the line provided, complete each sentence correctly by writing the contraction *don't* or *doesn't*.

> **EXAMPLE 1.** __*Doesn't*__ she want to go to the picnic with us?

1. The conductor of the orchestra _____ want to perform.

2. Gisela _____ want to continue the flute lessons.

3. _____ Nayati have a pen pal in the Philippines?

4. People _____ often refuse thanks for good deeds.

5. Chim _____ have a big part in the play.

6. _____ the Monteros have relatives in Costa Rica?

7. It simply _____ matter to me which movie we go to see.

8. The moon _____ look so large when it's low in the sky.

9. The people from the moving company _____ want to wait.

10. This ballpoint pen _____ look like mine.

Copyright © by Holt, Rinehart and Winston. All rights reserved.

WORKSHEET 6 | **Agreement of Subject and Verb (Rule 2 j)**

EXERCISE A   In each of the following sentences, draw one line under the subject and two lines under the correct verb form in parentheses.

> **EXAMPLE 1.** Here (*is, <u>are</u>*) the <u>castanets</u> that the dancers want to use.

1. There (*go, goes*) the ships with all their flags flying.
2. At the top of the hill (*stand, stands*) a beautiful, ancient pagoda.
3. Down the runway and out over the bay (*roar, roars*) the two jets.
4. There (*is, are*) not many nachos left on the platter.
5. (*Do, Does*) the children ever tire of playing soccer?
6. At the bottom of the rubbish heap (*was, were*) a box of valuable gems.
7. In front of their home (*stands, stand*) the totem pole that their grandfather carved.
8. There (*is, are*) only three clarinet players in the entire band.
9. (*Has, Have*) the preference of each member been expressed?
10. There (*was, were*) several moths hiding in the clothes closet.

EXERCISE B   Most of the following sentences contain an error in subject-verb agreement. Correct the error by crossing out the incorrect verb and writing the correct form on the line provided. For each sentence that is already correct, write *C*.

> **EXAMPLE** __*are*__ **1.** Where ~~is~~ the waffles for Uncle Findley's breakfast?

_____ 1. In an album on the top shelf is some of my drawings of the Inuit village.

_____ 2. Where is that book about José Martí?

_____ 3. There is several boys waiting for you on the front steps, Emilio.

_____ 4. Here at last was an opportunity for Lee to express herself.

_____ 5. Have one of the girls brought in the mail yet?

_____ 6. Here is the oranges you wanted.

_____ 7. There was too many raisins in that pudding for Maxine's taste.

_____ 8. Does either of your parents play mah-jongg?

_____ 9. On the beach beside the dock was three or four canoes.

_____ 10. There has been various explanations for the mayor's change of plans.

Copyright © by Holt, Rinehart and Winston. All rights reserved.

LANGUAGE HANDBOOK **2** **AGREEMENT**

WORKSHEET 7 | **Agreement of Subject and Verb (Rule 2 k)**

EXERCISE A   In each of the following sentences, underline the correct verb in parentheses.

> **EXAMPLE 1.** The cats (*don't*, *doesn't*) like fish.

1. Your books (*don't*, *doesn't*) interest me.

2. (*Don't*, *Doesn't*) he take karate lessons?

3. The elephant (*don't*, *doesn't*) forget.

4. The piñatas (*don't*, *doesn't*) weigh much.

5. He just (*don't*, *doesn't*) like to wash the dishes.

6. The oxen (*don't*, *doesn't*) eat enough.

7. They (*don't*, *doesn't*) usually ask directions.

8. The geese (*don't*, *doesn't*) fly.

9. She (*don't*, *doesn't*) have a computer yet.

10. The mouse (*don't*, *doesn't*) like the cheese.

EXERCISE B   Underline the subject of each of the following sentences. Then, on the line provided, complete each sentence correctly by writing the contraction *don't* or *doesn't*.

> **EXAMPLE 1.** A <u>can</u> of macadamia nuts <u>*doesn't*</u> last long at our house.

1. A bag of tortilla chips _____ make a balanced meal.

2. Aretha _____ want to miss the Kwanzaa celebration.

3. _____ everyone here like wild rice?

4. Julie's parents _____ let her watch television very often.

5. This book about Sojourner Truth _____ belong to me.

6. _____ the Tchong family live here anymore?

7. Those bikes across the street _____ belong to any of us.

8. _____ Martina Hingis win most of her tennis matches?

9. The rings of Saturn _____ look very clear in this photograph.

10. Omar _____ enjoy skating as much as we do.

Copyright © by Holt, Rinehart and Winston. All rights reserved.

LANGUAGE
HANDBOOK **2** **AGREEMENT**

WORKSHEET 8 | **Agreement of Subject and Verb (Rules 2 g–j, l–n)**

EXERCISE A In each of the following sentences, underline the correct verb in parentheses.

EXAMPLE 1. Linda Salvio and Pat Huggins (*enjoys*, <u>*enjoy*</u>) fishing.

1. Linda and Pat (*like*, *likes*) to go fishing at Lake Pewauskee.

2. Either Linda or Pat generally (*get*, *gets*) someone to take them out to the lake.

3. Then they and all the other anglers there (*spend*, *spends*) hours fishing.

4. Very often, Mr. Nakamoto and his grandson, Yori, (*is*, *are*) at the lake.

5. Both Mr. Nakamoto and Yori (*claim*, *claims*) that there are bass in that lake.

6. Neither Linda nor Pat (*has*, *have*) ever caught one, however.

7. Perhaps either the hook or the bait they use (*is*, *are*) no good.

8. At any rate, Linda and Pat freely (*admit*, *admits*) their failure at Lake Pewauskee.

9. Neither their lack of success nor the amount of time they have spent there (*keep*, *keeps*) them from going back to try again.

10. Some people from the city and even a few local residents (*think*, *thinks*) nothing of spending their whole vacation there.

EXERCISE B Most of the verb forms in the following sentences are incorrect. Cross out each incorrect verb, and write the correct form on the line provided. Write *C* for each verb form that is already correct.

EXAMPLE __*wants*__ **1.** Neither Eduardo nor his brother ~~want~~ to play golf.

_____ 1. The toy soldier and the kachina doll was placed on the top shelf.

_____ 2. A flood of letters have poured in since Monday.

_____ 3. Over thirty percent of the land are being set aside for parks.

_____ 4. Wales were the birthplace of Dylan Thomas.

_____ 5. Are the news on yet?

_____ 6. *The Education of Little Tree* and *Fly Away Home* is two movies I would recommend.

_____ 7. Mumps cause the enlargement of glands in the cheeks and neck.

_____ 8. Balsom Brothers Company produce party supplies.

_____ 9. The jury argues among themselves before reaching a verdict.

_____ 10. In seconds, seventy-five feet of fishing line disappears beneath the dark blue water as the shark speeds away.

Copyright © by Holt, Rinehart and Winston. All rights reserved.

Elements of Literature

WORKSHEET 9 **Pronoun-Antecedent Agreement (Rules 2 o–r)**

EXERCISE A For each of the following sentences, write an appropriate pronoun on the line provided.

> **EXAMPLE 1.** Our television is broken, and my mother says __*it*__ will not be fixed any time soon.

1. These Navajo blankets are special to us; _____ were made by my grandmother.

2. Thank you for helping Ms. Stevens and me; _____ will remember your kindness.

3. Joanne introduced me to _____ friends.

4. This is Mr. Hayakawa; please show _____ around our campus.

5. After Lynette Dyer Vuong learned Vietnamese, _____ translated a number of tales.

EXERCISE B Most of the following sentences contain pronouns that do not agree with their antecedents. Cross out any incorrect pronoun. Then, on the line provided, write the correct pronoun. If a sentence is already correct, write *C*.

> **EXAMPLE** __*they*__ **1.** Few in the balcony could hear, so ~~he or she~~ moved downstairs.

_____ **1.** No one should neglect their studies.

_____ **2.** Not all of the documentary was about Winston Churchill; they also contained footage about Franklin D. Roosevelt.

_____ **3.** Some of the sidewalk had chalk drawings on them.

_____ **4.** None of our horses have ever escaped its stalls.

_____ **5.** Both of the visitors arrived on time, and everything was ready for him or her.

_____ **6.** Everyone on the team must bring their own lunch.

_____ **7.** Any of these nails will do; they are all long enough.

_____ **8.** Do both of these messages go to Mr. Paul, or should Ms. Taylor see it too?

_____ **9.** Didn't most of these inventions use electricity for their power source?

_____ **10.** Several on the investigation team noticed the clue; what good detectives he or she were!

Copyright © by Holt, Rinehart and Winston. All rights reserved.

LANGUAGE HANDBOOK **2** AGREEMENT

WORKSHEET 10 Pronoun-Antecedent Agreement (Rules 2 s–x)

EXERCISE   For each of the following sentences, write an appropriate pronoun on the line provided.

EXAMPLE **1.** Betsy and Dan can't attend; __*they*__ are on vacation.

1. George Washington Carver and his students used the peanut plant for _____ experiments.

2. This batch of granola bars turned out pretty well, and _____ didn't cost much either.

3. Social studies may be simple for you, but I can't make sense of _____.

4. Either Mrs. Parquet or Miss Gant will wear _____ Dutch shoes to school next week.

5. After crossing the deep river, the posse stopped and emptied the water from _____ boots.

6. Lacey and Mateo miss _____ home in Puerto Rico.

7. Read *Wildflowers for Homes* because every plant in our area is in _____.

8. Take theater arts now because _____ won't be offered again this year.

9. I've saved six hundred dollars, and _____ is going toward a new computer.

10. The Confederacy seceded in 1860 and 1861. Name the states that belonged to _____.

11. Did the letter or the envelope have an address on _____?

12. Neither Sylvia nor Becky ran _____ best that day.

13. When did the Philippines form _____ current system of government?

14. This cluster of stars appears to be close to Earth, but millions of miles separate _____ from us.

15. If you have had mumps, you probably won't get _____ again.

16. After I spilled two cups of flour, I spent the next hour cleaning _____ up.

17. Although eight feet of mahogany wood will be expensive, _____ will be worth the cost.

18. We are reading John F. Kennedy's book *Profiles in Courage;* _____ has always been a favorite with students of history.

19. This Greek water jar and dish have scenes from Hercules' life on _____.

20. Neither Larry nor his brother remembered to wear _____ glasses.

Copyright © by Holt, Rinehart and Winston. All rights reserved.

| WORKSHEET 11 | Test (Rules 2 a–x) |

EXERCISE A   In each of the following sentences, circle the subject of the main clause and then underline the correct verb in parentheses.

> **EXAMPLE 1.** (Each) of these books (*was, were*) written by Nina Otero.

1. One of the Christmas tree ornaments (*is, are*) hand painted.

2. My passion for writing poems (*has, have*) grown since I read haiku by Matsuo Bashō.

3. (*Was, Were*) neither of the two orchestral pieces played well?

4. Everyone from the New England states (*is, are*) used to cold winters.

5. Three of the rarest coins in the collection (*was, were*) missing.

6. In my class, several of the students (*do, does*) play soccer well.

7. The light from the neon signs in the store windows (*is, are*) bright.

8. Everyone in our choral group (*love, loves*) to sing "I Got Rhythm."

9. Measles (*is, are*) very rare today, but doctors see a few cases of the disease each year.

10. Anyone with a desire to play and with patience enough to practice (*make, makes*) a good piano student.

11. In the center of each table (*sit, sits*) a bowl of fresh flowers.

12. Where (*was, were*) the other members of the committee during the meeting?

13. Seven dollars and forty cents (*was, were*) refunded to me by mail for the broken picture frame.

14. (*Has, Have*) Lisa or Margrit read the poems by Langston Hughes?

15. The class (*take, takes*) four bus routes to school from different parts of town.

16. Alfie and Louise sometimes (*do, does*) their volunteer work together.

17. (*Don't, Doesn't*) several of you leave for camp tomorrow?

18. Copies of the novel by Gary Soto (*is, are*) on my desk.

19. Neither Ethel nor her friends (*want, wants*) to leave.

20. Behind the marching band (*come, comes*) a few of the most elaborate floats.

21. "Amigo Brothers" (*is, are*) assigned for reading and discussion on Friday.

22. Neither of the puppies (*was, were*) housebroken.

23. Most of the club members (*has, have*) received awards for community service.

24. Each of the boys (*was, were*) praised for his sportsmanship.

25. The solutions to the mysteries surrounding the crimes (*was, were*) given by the detective.

Continued ☞

Copyright © by Holt, Rinehart and Winston. All rights reserved.

EXERCISE B   On the line provided for each of the following sentences, write a pronoun that is in the same gender and number as its antecedent. Then, underline the antecedent.

EXAMPLE **1.** <u>Patricia</u> has ___*her*___ gloves.

1. The choreographer Debbie Allen directed the dancers and the singers to take _____ places.

2. Everyone has _____ assignment.

3. Pete and Stu are feeding _____ palominos and the other horses.

4. Neither Sally nor Lucy has brought _____ sitar.

5. The teachers attended _____ meeting.

6. Each of the girls knows _____ lines.

7. Someone left _____ umbrella here.

8. Dad likes _____ new key chain.

9. Taos, New Mexico, is famous for _____ art colony.

10. Each of the boys fixed _____ own bike.

EXERCISE C   Most of the following sentences contain pronouns that do not agree with their antecedents. Cross out each incorrect pronoun. Then, on the line provided, write the correct pronoun. If a sentence is already correct, write *C*.

EXAMPLE ___*it*___ **1.** Although *Sylvester and the Magic Pebble* won the Caldecott Medal many years ago, today's children still love ~~them~~.

_____ **1.** Several of the stones had strange markings on it.

_____ **2.** The Netherlands reclaimed two fifths of their land from the North Sea.

_____ **3.** I hope you saw the news last night; we were on them!

_____ **4.** Alarmed, the herd of gazelles scattered when it scented the lions.

_____ **5.** All of the designers used variations on this curve for their doors.

_____ **6.** Few of the students knew his or her locker combinations yet.

_____ **7.** Mathematics must be your favorite subject; you've been studying them for hours.

_____ **8.** Join Students for Bike Trails today at 3:45 when it meets in the cafeteria.

_____ **9.** One by one, the band got its instruments out of the bus and headed for the field.

_____ **10.** Do any of these pizzas have anchovies on it?

Copyright © by Holt, Rinehart and Winston. All rights reserved.

LANGUAGE HANDBOOK **3** **USING VERBS**

WORKSHEET 1 **Using Regular and Irregular Verbs (Rules 3 a–c)**

EXERCISE A For each of the following sentences, write the correct past or past participle form of the verb in italics.

EXAMPLE *sail* **1.** Few people have __*sailed*__ the seven seas.

lack **1.** Julius Caesar _____ nothing except true friendship.

form **2.** Giant stone beams _____ doorways in the ancient Mayan ruins.

register **3.** Have you _____ for the skateboard contest?

guard **4.** For centuries, this precious well in the Arabian Desert has been _____ carefully.

whistle **5.** Her parrot _____ the theme song of *Star Trek,* and he wouldn't stop!

EXERCISE B For each of the following sentences, write the correct past or past participle form of the verb in italics.

EXAMPLE *set* **1.** Have you __*set*__ the table yet?

hurt **1.** Oddly, competition has not _____ our sales.

know **2.** He _____ everything there was to know about automobile engines.

catch **3.** The hero Bellerophon _____ Pegasus, the flying horse.

swing **4.** John Henry _____ a sledgehammer.

swim **5.** Who first _____ across the English Channel?

cost **6.** Julius Caesar's great power had _____ him his life.

begin **7.** Who can tell me when the Chinese calendar _____?

lead **8.** Proudly, Mr. Bowers _____ the prize filly around the ring.

put **9.** When I came in, I _____ the mail on the hall table.

hold **10.** Throughout the storm, the captain had _____ the ship steady.

hit **11.** Yikes! I must have accidentally _____ the delete key!

go **12.** She _____ to the grocery store for milk and bread.

choose **13.** Which door should the contestant have _____?

say **14.** Yesterday, he _____ he'd be here.

spread **15.** Rats _____ the bubonic plague throughout Europe.

Copyright © by Holt, Rinehart and Winston. All rights reserved.

Continued ☞

get   **16.** A stray bolt _____ into the gears, bringing the machine to a halt.

do   **17.** They have _____ all they can to help the baby squirrels get back in their nest.

send   **18.** Has she _____ in her entry yet?

sing   **19.** When we were in Germany, people often _____ in restaurants and in train stations.

let   **20.** Who has _____ the hamsters out again?

EXERCISE C   Each of the following sentences contains an error in the use of verbs. Cross out each error. Then, on the line provided, write the correct verb.

EXAMPLE   _brought_   **1.** Who ~~brung~~ these flowers?

_____ **1.** The question remains: Who builded the pyramids?

_____ **2.** Oh, no! The baby has drawed all over the walls!

_____ **3.** Ladies and gentlemen, Stokes has broke his own record!

_____ **4.** How long has earth spinned on its axis?

_____ **5.** I should have knowed better.

_____ **6.** When Garry slided into home with the winning run, the crowd roared.

_____ **7.** I think that bee just stinged me.

_____ **8.** Wait until you hear what Leslie just telled me about her vacation!

_____ **9.** Craig has already spended his allowance, so he can't go to the movies with us.

_____ **10.** If you had buyed that T-shirt, you wouldn't have had enough money left for a CD.

Copyright © by Holt, Rinehart and Winston. All rights reserved.

LANGUAGE HANDBOOK **3** **USING VERBS**

WORKSHEET 2 **Irregular Verbs (Rule 3 c)**

EXERCISE For each of the following sentences, write, on the line provided, the correct past or past participle form of the verb in italics.

> **EXAMPLE** *choose* **1.** Nina ___chose___ to buy a print of a painting by Grandma Moses.

build **1.** My uncle has _____ a playhouse for my little sister.

choose **2.** He had _____ to read Rodolfo Anaya's book *Bless Me, Ultima*.

blow **3.** For my little brother's birthday party, I must have _____ up a hundred balloons.

freeze **4.** Haven't you ever _____ juice for snacks?

steal **5.** Toni Braxton had _____ the show.

give **6.** Would you have _____ them another chance?

ride **7.** Ynes Mexia _____ a balsa raft on one of her botanical expeditions.

fall **8.** Every good rider has _____ at least once.

lead **9.** Ms. Johnson _____ the discussion about the Langston Hughes poem.

break **10.** Armand dropped his watch and _____ it.

throw **11.** Carlos wound up and _____ the ball with all his might.

eat **12.** Have you ever _____ octopus or squid?

speak **13.** The lecturer had _____ on the same subject before.

have **14.** Even ancient peoples _____ a good understanding of the moon's phases.

drive **15.** They _____ the cattle along the Chisholm Trail.

be **16.** Last week I _____ riding on a float in the Cinco de Mayo parade!

take **17.** Demetrius has _____ first prize for cooking.

write **18.** Louisa May Alcott _____ many stories before *Little Women* was published in 1868.

swim **19.** We have _____ in the pond often.

put **20.** Where have you _____ your report on the Underground Railroad?

wear **21.** The ceremonial dresses that they _____ are now in a museum.

let **22.** We stowed our paddles and _____ the current take us downstream.

come **23.** Oops, the paper streamers have _____ down.

do **24.** Charlotte _____ her project on the Iroquois Confederacy.

see **25.** I _____ four possums and a deer over in the woods.

Copyright © by Holt, Rinehart and Winston. All rights reserved.

LANGUAGE
HANDBOOK **3** **USING VERBS**

| WORKSHEET 3 | **Irregular Verbs (Rule 3 c)**

EXERCISE A   For each of the following sentences, write, on the line provided, the correct past or past participle form of the verb in italics.

EXAMPLE *give* **1.** My aunt Tena ___*gave*___ me a turquoise bracelet.

do   **1.** By noon, we had _____ everything on the chores list.

know   **2.** She had _____ Princess Diana for many years.

throw   **3.** Francesca had _____ the ball without looking carefully.

draw   **4.** My brother _____ pictures of everyone he knows.

wear   **5.** The pencil was _____ down to a stub.

read   **6.** Have you ever _____ the speech by Cayuga Chief Logan?

cut   **7.** Razor-sharp coral had _____ right through our sneakers.

catch   **8.** In one short hour, Frank _____ skiing fever, and he's been on the slopes ever since.

blow   **9.** The Sherpa guide _____ on his hands to keep them warm.

bring   **10.** Let me show you the dancer's mask that Dad _____ me from Mexico.

EXERCISE B   For the following sentences, cross out each incorrect verb form and write the correct form on the line provided. If the verb form is already correct, write *C*.

EXAMPLE ___*gave*___ **1.** Lucas ~~gived~~ me a bicycle helmet for my birthday.

_____ **1.** By the time we got there, they had already went to the picnic.

_____ **2.** He had never ran so hard in all his life.

_____ **3.** Climbing up the tree, Tomás torn his poncho.

_____ **4.** Too late, I discovered that the bag of cornmeal had bursted.

_____ **5.** Later that night, the Inuit games begun.

_____ **6.** Geronimo had chose his homeland and would take no other.

_____ **7.** Wow! The President has send Uncle Jake a birthday card!

_____ **8.** Has any singer ever held a note as long as he?

_____ **9.** It's a wonder your band hasn't shaked the house down.

_____ **10.** Whitney Houston has sang on stage, on video, and in the movies.

Copyright © by Holt, Rinehart and Winston. All rights reserved.

LANGUAGE HANDBOOK **3** USING VERBS

| WORKSHEET 4 | Using *Sit* and *Set* Correctly (Rule 3 c)

EXERCISE A   On the line provided for each of the following sentences, write the letter *a* or *b* to show the meaning of the italicized verb:

> *a*—means "to rest in an upright, seated position"
>
> *b*—means "to put (something) in a place"

> EXAMPLES __*a*__ **1.** The paint bucket was *sitting* on the top shelf.
>
> __*b*__ **2.** She *set* the bonsai in front of the window.

_____ **1.** Mrs. Petersen *sits* in this chair while she reads.

_____ **2.** Mountain climbers often *set* a flag on the summit of a peak.

_____ **3.** We *set* the vase of roses on the table.

_____ **4.** "Someone," said the bear, "has been *sitting* in my chair!"

_____ **5.** Please *set* the dish of fruit on the table.

_____ **6.** Floyd *set* his glasses on the end of his nose and went to work.

_____ **7.** The small Persian kitten was *sitting* beside me on the sofa.

_____ **8.** I couldn't have *sat* there another minute.

_____ **9.** We *sat* in the waiting room for two hours.

_____ **10.** Pedro *sets* his in-line skates next to mine.

EXERCISE B   For each of the following sentences, underline the correct verb form in parentheses.

> EXAMPLE **1.** The server (*sat*, *set*) a basket of fresh flatbread on the buffet.

1. My dog (*sits*, *sets*) in the shade in the afternoon.

2. Hearing a floorboard creak, Meredith (*sat*, *set*) up in bed.

3. The writer (*sat*, *set*) down and began to write about the Taino people of the West Indies.

4. (*Sit*, *Set*) the books there, and I will put them away.

5. Does this machine (*sit*, *set*) up the bowling pins automatically?

6. Beatrice (*sat*, *set*) down on the porch swing and began reading a novel.

7. She was still (*sitting*, *setting*) there an hour later.

8. Angelo (*sat*, *set*) his box of baseball cards in his locker.

9. Juanita and I (*sit*, *set*) in the front of the class.

10. (*Sit*, *Set*) the basket of mangoes in the back of the truck.

Copyright © by Holt, Rinehart and Winston. All rights reserved.

Elements of Literature   *Using Verbs* **31**

LANGUAGE HANDBOOK 3 USING VERBS

| WORSHEET 5 | Using *Lie* and *Lay* Correctly (Rule 3 c)

EXERCISE A   On the line provided for each of the following sentences, write the letter *a* or *b* to show the meaning of the italicized verb:

> *a*—means "to rest, to recline, or to be in a place"

> *b*—means "to put (something) in a place"

EXAMPLES __*a*__ **1.** On Saturdays I often *lie* in bed until ten o'clock.

__*b*__ **2.** The contractor is already *laying* the foundation for our new school.

_____ **1.** Isabella *lay* on the sand and watched the waves.

_____ **2.** Alex *laid* his sunglasses on his towel and went for a swim.

_____ **3.** Cuba *lies* south of Florida.

_____ **4.** Is her bike *lying* in the snow?

_____ **5.** The donkey has *lain* down and will not get up.

_____ **6.** The children had *laid* their stockings by the fireplace.

_____ **7.** The farmhouse *lies* at the foot of the next hill.

_____ **8.** In the evening Miles *lays* out his clothes for the next day.

_____ **9.** My report on the life of Barbara Jordan is *lying* on the kitchen table.

_____ **10.** The major saluted and *laid* the report on the general's desk.

EXERCISE B   For each sentence, underline the correct verb form in parentheses.

EXAMPLE **1.** Mario's drawing is (*laying*, *lying*) on his chair.

1. If Jorge (*lies*, *lays*) there much longer, he may get a sunburn.

2. Mother and I had already (*lain*, *laid*) our plans for the surprise party.

3. Ms. Nesbitt (*laid*, *lay*) a copy of the play on each student's desk.

4. Several bags of recyclable cans and bottles are (*laying*, *lying*) in our garage.

5. The clothes had (*lain*, *laid*) too long in the sun and had faded.

6. The inn (*lay*, *laid*) near where the village store once stood.

7. (*Lie*, *Lay*) the flowers on the monument.

8. At the bottom of the hole (*lay*, *laid*) a tin box of old papers.

9. A heap of rusty metal was (*lying*, *laying*) beside the barn.

10. I. M. Pei, the talented architect, (*lay*, *laid*) the building plans on the table.

Copyright © by Holt, Rinehart and Winston. All rights reserved.

Elements of Literature

LANGUAGE HANDBOOK **3** **USING VERBS**

WORKSHEET 6 Using *Rise* and *Raise* Correctly (Rule 3 c)

EXERCISE A For each of the following sentences, underline the correct verb in parentheses.

EXAMPLE 1. Is the tide still (*raising*, *rising*)?

1. Our cat always (*raises, rises*) quite slowly when his name is called.

2. That was the only time my father ever (*rose, raised*) his voice.

3. (*Raise, Rise*) the anchor; we're bound for Sydney!

4. Will bread dough (*raise, rise*) in cold weather?

5. A fresh wind (*raised, rose*), filling our sails.

6. I was just (*raising, rising*) the blinds when the phone rang.

7. How could the Easter Islanders have (*raised, risen*) those huge stones?

8. Look! Tiny seedlings are (*raising, rising*) from the potting soil.

9. A complex system of locks (*raises, rises*) the water level of the Panama Canal.

10. Test scores have (*raised, risen*) for three years in a row.

EXERCISE B For each of the following sentences, write the correct form of *rise* or *raise*.

EXAMPLE 1. Kim was the only one who __*raised*__ his hand.

1. As we watched, a deer's antlers _____ above the brush.

2. What forces cause the mercury in a thermometer to _____ and lower?

3. With a word from the sentry, the guard _____ the gate, and the jeep passed through.

4. Only four very strong men could have _____ such a huge log.

5. Gratefully, we watched as the hand of the gas gauge _____ to "full."

6. In a few minutes, the balloons had _____ out of sight.

7. As the warm front passes through, the temperature will _____.

8. Every morning I watch the sun _____ over the mountains.

9. Once again, his words had _____ our hopes and our spirits.

10. Did pirates really _____ the Jolly Roger?

Copyright © by Holt, Rinehart and Winston. All rights reserved.

LANGUAGE HANDBOOK 3 USING VERBS

WORKSHEET 7 Verb Tense (Rule 3 d)

EXERCISE A   The verbs in each of the following sentences are printed in italics. On the line provided, write *present* if the verb expresses action taking place in the present, or write *past* if the verb expresses action taking place in the past.

> EXAMPLE __past__ **1.** Who *won* medals at the 1998 Winter Olympics in Nagano, Japan?

_____ **1.** She *is taking* figure skating lessons.

_____ **2.** We *watched* the Winter Olympics on television.

_____ **3.** Michelle Kwan *competed* for a medal.

_____ **4.** We *saw* Michelle skate once before.

_____ **5.** On the ice rink, the figure skater *was applauded* loudly.

_____ **6.** She *glides* over the ice gracefully.

_____ **7.** Ski jumping also *interested* us.

_____ **8.** The ski jumpers *are soaring* into the air.

_____ **9.** They *control* the flight of their jumps.

_____ **10.** *Was* the ski jumper Masahiko Harada *competing* last winter?

EXERCISE B   The italicized verb in each of the following sentences expresses either present or past time. On the lines provided, write the present tense form of each past tense verb and the past tense form of each present tense verb.

> EXAMPLE __cares__ **1.** Squeaky, the main character of the story, *cared* for her brother, Raymond.

_____ **1.** He *serves* as an ambassador to South Africa.

_____ **2.** The commanding officer *earned* their respect.

_____ **3.** Julia Child *baked* a superb apple dessert.

_____ **4.** I *pour* too much milk on my cereal.

_____ **5.** We *enjoy* our new book by Virginia Hamilton.

_____ **6.** A few swimmers *used* a spray to keep off the mosquitoes.

_____ **7.** At my desk I *work* on my homework assignment.

_____ **8.** Jerry *visited* Mexico in the winter.

_____ **9.** Nataliya Makarova *dances* beautifully.

_____ **10.** Peter *plays* a good chess game.

Copyright © by Holt, Rinehart and Winston. All rights reserved.

Elements of Literature

LANGUAGE HANDBOOK **3** **USING VERBS**

WORKSHEET 8 **Consistency of Verb Tense (Rule 3 e)**

EXERCISE A   Read the following paragraph, and decide whether you want to use the present tense or the past tense to rewrite the paragraph. Then, on the lines provided, rewrite the paragraph, changing the verb forms to make the verb tenses consistent.

EXAMPLE [1] Aunt Irene visits Japan and sent me a package.

Aunt Irene visited Japan and sent me a package.
or
Aunt Irene visits Japan and sends me a package.

[1] I come home from school, and there on the doorstep was a package. [2] I run inside and broke the string. [3] My mom came in and sits down with me. [4] In the package was a silky blue kimono, which I take out carefully. [5] Something else is hidden inside—a set of delicate teacups, which I placed on the table. [6] I dug through the shredded newspapers and find a box of tea, so Mom went into the kitchen and makes some tea. [7] At the very bottom lies Aunt Irene's letter; in it, she taught me a little about fans. [8] Later, I wear the kimono, and Mom and I drank from the cups. [9] We took a picture of me for Aunt Irene; then, I write a thank-you note and told her all about school. [10] My aunt's gift was very thoughtful, and I am glad she does not forget me.

_____

_____

_____

_____

_____

_____

_____

_____

_____

_____

_____

_____

_____

Continued ☞

Copyright © by Holt, Rinehart and Winston. All rights reserved.

EXERCISE B   Read the following paragraph, and decide whether you want to rewrite it in the present tense or the past tense. Then, on the lines provided, rewrite the paragraph, changing the verb forms to make them consistent with the tense you choose.

EXAMPLE [1] When I was in Hawaii, I see many people surfing the waves.

When I am in Hawaii, I see many people surfing the waves.
or
When I was in Hawaii, I saw many people surfing the waves.

[1] Some of the surfers were very good, but others look like beginners. [2] I hear that good surfers needed excellent timing and reflexes. [3] They also needed to anticipate a wave's action. [4] The surfers use two kinds of boards when they rode the waves. [5] Shortboards are those under seven feet long; longboards were those over seven feet. [6] Surfers lie or knelt on the board and paddle out to where the waves began to break. [7] When a wave started to move to shore, the surfers paddle to a spot just ahead of the wave. [8] When the wave started to lift the board, the surfers stand up. [9] The surfers shifted their weight to steer the board along the smooth water just below the top of the wave. [10] Expert surfers had to be in excellent physical shape when they perform difficult, exciting moves.

_____

_____

_____

_____

_____

_____

_____

_____

_____

_____

_____

Copyright © by Holt, Rinehart and Winston. All rights reserved.

LANGUAGE HANDBOOK **3** USING VERBS

WORSHEET 9	Test (Rules 3 a–d)

EXERCISE A   On the lines provided, write the past and the past participle forms of the following verbs.

	PAST	PAST PARTICIPLE
EXAMPLE eat	**1.** _____ate_____	_____eaten_____

	PAST	PAST PARTICIPLE			PAST	PAST PARTICIPLE
break	**1.** _____	_____	rise	**11.** _____	_____
give	**2.** _____	_____	freeze	**12.** _____	_____
lead	**3.** _____	_____	take	**13.** _____	_____
like	**4.** _____	_____	say	**14.** _____	_____
throw	**5.** _____	_____	know	**15.** _____	_____
catch	**6.** _____	_____	set	**16.** _____	_____
hold	**7.** _____	_____	raise	**17.** _____	_____
speak	**8.** _____	_____	shake	**18.** _____	_____
jump	**9.** _____	_____	draw	**19.** _____	_____
build	**10.** _____	_____	swing	**20.** _____	_____

EXERCISE B   For each of the following sentences, underline the correct verb form in parentheses.

EXAMPLE 1. Have you (*saw, <u>seen</u>*) the film *The Autobiography of Miss Jane Pittman*?

1. The guests have (*drank, drunk*) all of the apple juice.

2. We (*saw, seen*) you at LeAnn Rimes's concert.

3. Last night, the children (*ran, run*) around the yard, chasing fireflies.

4. Carlos's aunt has (*drove, driven*) here from Durango, Mexico.

5. She has (*tore, torn*) two pages out of the notebook.

6. The kayak (*hit, hitted*) a rock, and the campers fell into the water.

7. The wind has (*blew, blown*) the shutter open.

Continued ☞

Copyright © by Holt, Rinehart and Winston. All rights reserved.

8. We had (*rode, ridden*) overnight on the bus to Yoho National Park in British Columbia.

9. Before the weekend is over, Marla will have (*went, gone*) to the library to find information on the life of Dr. Martin Luther King, Jr.

10. The courageous woman has (*swam, swum*) all the way across Lake Erie.

11. I have (*wrote, written*) a report about Red Cloud, a leader of the Oglala Sioux.

12. By tomorrow, you will have (*sang, sung*) the national anthem in front of one thousand people.

13. They certainly have (*took, taken*) their time preparing the quesadillas.

14. The picture was (*stole, stolen*) some time before 11:00 P.M.

15. The basset hound was (*lying, laying*) under the tree, sound asleep.

16. Why don't you (*sit, set*) down and stay awhile?

17. Have you (*brung, brought*) the newspaper in yet?

18. The explorers were miles from their camp when it (*began, begun*) to snow.

19. Brenda set the shoes she had (*wore, worn*) near the fire.

20. The vase has (*fell, fallen*) off the table.

EXERCISE C   In each of the following sentences, cross out the incorrect verb form, and write the correct past form of the verb on the line provided. *Note:* Do not cross out any helping verbs.

EXAMPLE ___*gone*___ **1.** Jacinto, Angela, and I had ~~went~~ to the craft show, hoping to learn some new skills.

_____ **1.** We buyed our own materials for the crafts in which we were interested.

_____ **2.** Jacinto wanted to learn how wool is spinned.

_____ **3.** The wool spinners sended Angela to see the weavers.

_____ **4.** She wanted to pick up some tips on how colors should be chose for the best effect.

_____ **5.** I had came to the show to learn about stained-glass construction.

_____ **6.** I had already made two small pieces, which I lay proudly on the table.

_____ **7.** We had watch a silk-screen artist at work in another craft show.

_____ **8.** After the committee member had spoke, we accompanied the artists to their work areas.

_____ **9.** They done their best to help us.

_____ **10.** Some selled us fine examples of their work.

Copyright © by Holt, Rinehart and Winston. All rights reserved.

NAME _____ CLASS _____ DATE _____

LANGUAGE HANDBOOK 4 USING PRONOUNS

WORKSHEET 1 | **The Nominative Case (Rule 4 a)**

EXERCISE A For each sentence, write, on the line provided, an appropriate personal pronoun in the nominative case. Use a variety of pronouns, but do not use *you* or *it*.

EXAMPLE 1. ___*We*___ listened to General Colin Powell's speech.

1. Grace and _____ are officers of the Ecology Club.

2. _____ and Clayton are avid soccer fans.

3. Are _____ and _____ tied for first place?

4. Last week, Pia and _____ watched the Harlem Globetrotters play basketball.

5. _____ studied the life of Chief Joseph, a leader of the Nez Perce.

6. _____ and _____ always forget their books.

7. Danny and _____ lost our way, but our teacher and _____ found us.

8. _____ gave me a recipe for *enchiladas verdes*.

9. Both _____ and Margaret Mead were anthropologists.

10. _____ hopes to compete in the Summer Olympics in 2004.

EXERCISE B Complete each of the following sentences by writing, on the line provided, the nominative-case personal pronouns described in parentheses.

EXAMPLE 1. ___*He*___ and Michael Chang were the finalists.
(*third person singular, masculine*)

1. _____ and Roberta left for Rome last night. (*third person singular, feminine*)

2. _____ hope to see some kangaroos and koalas in the wild. (*third person plural*)

3. Norman, Claude, and _____ camped out overnight. (*first person singular*)

4. Are you or _____ planning to go to college? (*third person singular, masculine*)

5. Maggie, Miss Klein, and _____ are traveling together. (*third person plural*)

6. _____ have memorized the poem "Pueblo Winter." (*first person singular*)

7. _____ and _____ are making posters for Hispanic Heritage Month.
(*third person singular, masculine; first person singular*)

8. _____ and _____ were wearing identical hats. (*third person singular, feminine; first person singular*)

9. Both _____ and _____ are tae kwon do instructors. (*third person singular, feminine; third person singular, masculine*)

10. _____ left the kibbutz in 1996 but returned to the farm four years later. (*first person plural*)

Copyright © by Holt, Rinehart and Winston. All rights reserved.

LANGUAGE HANDBOOK **4** USING PRONOUNS

WORKSHEET 2 | The Nominative Case (Rule 4 b)

EXERCISE A   In each of the following sentences, underline the correct form of the personal pronouns in parentheses.

> **EXAMPLE 1.** Was it (<u>*he*</u>, *him*) or Tiger Woods who won the golf tournament?

1. The club president next year will be (*she, her*).

2. The last guests to arrive were Julius and (*her, she*).

3. Were the winners (*them, they*) and (*we, us*)?

4. The finalist might be either you or (*her, she*).

5. The two fastest runners were Michael Johnson and (*she, her*).

6. The founders of the Journalism Club were (*them, they*) and (*us, we*).

7. Was it (*she, her*) or Rebecca that you talked to on the train?

8. It might possibly have been (*him, he*) whom you met.

9. Was it Nancy Lopez or (*she, her*) who was ahead?

10. It will be (*he, him*), (*her, she*), or (*I, me*) who will be chosen.

EXERCISE B   Proofread each of the following sentences. Cross out any incorrect pronoun, and on the line provided, write the correct pronoun. If a sentence is already correct, write *C*.

> **EXAMPLE** ___/___ **1.** Will the next one up to bat be ~~me~~?

_____ **1.** One of the ones who saw the future of Kenya was him, Jomo Kenyatta.

_____ **2.** Nobody knew that the clowns were us!

_____ **3.** I thought the treasurer of the Chess Club would be her.

_____ **4.** The only two left in the testing room were Ethan and I.

_____ **5.** Melissa said those people by the door were the mayor and them.

_____ **6.** Why couldn't the ones on stage have been us?

_____ **7.** Wasn't that your mother and her?

_____ **8.** Yes, that was him on the phone.

_____ **9.** Next year, the one with the blue ribbon will be me.

_____ **10.** Could it have been them in the red convertible?

Copyright © by Holt, Rinehart and Winston. All rights reserved.

LANGUAGE HANDBOOK **4** **USING PRONOUNS**

WORKSHEET 3 **The Objective Case (Rules 4 c, d)**

EXERCISE A On the line provided for each of the following sentences, write an appropriate personal pronoun in the objective case. Use a variety of pronouns, but do not use *you* or *it*.

EXAMPLE 1. Roberto called ___me___ from Puebla, Mexico.

1. Luisa brought _____ a tape from the video store.

2. The president appointed _____ to the budget committee.

3. We lent their friends and _____ our lacrosse sticks.

4. The pass play fooled the coach and _____.

5. Hui Chun directed _____ to the media center.

6. I signaled Carrie and _____ from the next hill.

7. The principal recognized _____ for our contributions to the school's Earth Day activities.

8. Phyllis gave Gardner and _____ pictures of the pyramids of San Juan Teotihuacán.

9. During the night, mosquitoes kept Marty and _____ awake.

10. Mr. Salisbury will drive _____ to the soccer game.

EXERCISE B For each of the following sentences, underline the correct pronoun form in parentheses.

EXAMPLE 1. The Hsing family asked (*we, us*) to the Chinese New Year celebration.

1. Mrs. Lowell praised Louis and (*I, me*) for our work.

2. No, the storm did not worry (*she, her*) or (*I, me*).

3. Who gave (*them, they*) the inspiration for this play?

4. His pet Pomeranian never leaves (*he, him*) alone for a minute.

5. The story about the UFO frightened both (*him, he*) and (*me, I*).

6. Tell Amber and (*we, us*) a story about the old days, Grandma!

7. Vinnie Orlando invited Sheila and (*I, me*) to the dress rehearsal of the musical *West Side Story*.

8. The photographs of Mars amazed not only (*them, they*) but also the NASA scientists.

9. Why don't you draw (*they, them*) a map of how to get to the science museum?

10. Neither Shirley nor Seymour had seen (*her, she*) before.

Copyright © by Holt, Rinehart and Winston. All rights reserved.

LANGUAGE HANDBOOK **4** **USING PRONOUNS**

WORKSHEET 4 **The Objective Case (Rule 4 e)**

EXERCISE A   In each of the following sentences, underline the prepositional phrase and circle the correct pronoun in parentheses.

> **EXAMPLE** **1.** I have been talking <u>to Emilio and (*he,* ⟨*him*⟩)</u>.

1. My aunt Anita brought gifts for my brother and (*I, me*).

2. We were sitting behind Olivia and (*him, he*).

3. Red Cloud stood proudly before (*they, them*) and spoke eloquently.

4. Has anyone heard from the Morgans and (*they, them*)?

5. The bus left without our teacher and (*us, we*).

6. I have confidence in Coach Stamos and (*them, they*).

7. We agreed to stay near the Shoshone guide and (*she, her*).

8. The others gathered around Terry and (*me, I*).

9. The children went with Jane and (*she, her*).

10. There was no agreement between Silvio and (*me, I*).

EXERCISE B   Most of the following sentences contain errors in the use of pronouns. Cross out each incorrect pronoun and write the correct form. Write *C* if a sentence is correct.

> **EXAMPLE** ___*him*___ **1.** Were these short stories written by ~~he~~ or by Melvin?

_____ **1.** Nothing was too difficult for Russell and I.

_____ **2.** The present was delivered to me, but it was really for he.

_____ **3.** Nicky and she suddenly arrived with both of them.

_____ **4.** Except for the Russoffs and we, nobody knew the hiding place.

_____ **5.** Seymour sat down between Mickey and she.

_____ **6.** The two Siberian huskies raced past Wallace and he.

_____ **7.** The rain poured down like a waterfall on Rosa, Madeline, and I.

_____ **8.** Dad and he were playing the game with Uncle Godfrey and they.

_____ **9.** Karen wrote a story about the relationship between the Ojibwa nation and they.

_____ **10.** Searching for Medusa, Perseus received help from both he and the Greek goddess Athena.

Copyright © by Holt, Rinehart and Winston. All rights reserved.

LANGUAGE HANDBOOK **4** USING PRONOUNS

WORKSHEET 5 | Special Pronoun Problems (Rule 4)

EXERCISE A For each of the following sentences, underline the correct pronoun in parentheses.

EXAMPLE 1. Yes, (_we_, _us_) Girl Scouts often go camping.

1. Choosing colors is easy for (_we_, _us_) artists.
2. Mr. Ekoomiak told (_we_, _us_) neighbors stories about his days as a bush pilot in Alaska.
3. (_We_, _Us_) folk dancers always do our best during performances.
4. The leaders of the parade will be (_we_, _us_) majorettes.
5. Hooray! Grandma knitted (_we_, _us_) girls new sweaters.
6. Shouldn't the opening act be (_we_, _us_) chorus members?
7. Will (_we_, _us_) Spanish students be entering the speech contest this year?
8. Are you coming with (_we_, _us_) kids to the Museum of Science and Industry?
9. Will you take (_we_, _us_) seventh-graders to the state capitol this year?
10. At the end of class, the coach handed (_we_, _us_) wrestlers a copy of the rules.

EXERCISE B On the line provided, write the appropriate reflexive pronoun for each of the following sentences.

EXAMPLE 1. Write __*yourself*__ a note so that you won't forget.

1. My little sister always sings _____ to sleep.
2. You Scouts ought to be proud of _____.
3. Actually, we taught _____ how to build a stage set.
4. You could have saved _____ a lot of trouble.
5. I promised _____ a bowl of popcorn tonight.
6. The children prepared a lunch for _____.
7. Jim decided he could move the box _____.
8. Surely, you aren't going to the movie by _____.
9. I thought to _____ that it was a beautiful day.
10. Will Bill and Joan be able to get _____ ready on time?

Continued ☞

Copyright © by Holt, Rinehart and Winston. All rights reserved.

EXERCISE C   Each of the following sentences contains a pronoun that is used incorrectly. Cross out each incorrect pronoun. Then, on the line provided, write the correct pronoun.

EXAMPLE ___*himself*___ **1.** He insists on doing everything for ~~hisself~~.

_____   **1.** Hey, Rick has bought hisself a new bike!

_____   **2.** Some girls built theirself a treehouse in the tree behind our house.

_____   **3.** He'll push hisself harder at the state track meet.

_____   **4.** After school, they fixed theirselves a few sandwiches.

_____   **5.** Well, they certainly made theirself at home.

EXERCISE D   Some of the following sentences contain errors in the use of *who* and *whom*. Cross out each error. Then, on the line provided, write the correct pronoun. If a sentence is already correct, write *C*.

EXAMPLE ___*who*___ **1.** No one knows ~~whom~~ made these ancient structures.

_____   **1.** Whom will be the first woman on the moon?

_____   **2.** Tim, by whom was the Declaration of Independence written?

_____   **3.** For who or what is California named?

_____   **4.** Mom, whom was at the door?

_____   **5.** Mr. Carl, whom were Frederick Douglass's heroes?

_____   **6.** Who should I ask about early reservations?

_____   **7.** Who modeled for the Statue of Liberty?

_____   **8.** Whom will hide the Easter eggs this year?

_____   **9.** Whom gave you that idea?

_____   **10.** With who did Meriwether Lewis travel?

Copyright © by Holt, Rinehart and Winston. All rights reserved.

WORKSHEET 6	Test (Rules 4 a–e)

EXERCISE A   In each of the following sentences, identify the use of each italicized pronoun by writing, on the line provided, *S* for subject, *PN* for predicate nominative, *DO* for direct object, or *OP* for object of a preposition. (Some sentences contain two pronouns to identify.)

EXAMPLE   <u>_PN_</u>   **1.** If ever there were a born turtle lover, it is *I*.

_____ **1.** *I* like studying about turtles.

_____ **2.** Why do *you* think turtles are fascinating?

_____ **3.** The sizes of turtles interest *me*.

_____ **4.** Today's turtles seem extremely small if *you* compare *them* to their extinct relatives.

_____ **5.** Nevertheless, many of today's turtles would seem very large to *you*.

_____ **6.** One such species consists of the leatherback turtles; *it* is *they* who achieve enormous sizes.

_____ **7.** The shells of hawksbill turtles are covered by hard plates; many of *them* were used to make tortoise-shell ornaments.

_____ **8.** My mother has an antique tortoise-shell comb that her grandmother gave to *her*.

_____ **9.** *She* knows that hawksbill turtles are rare today.

_____ **10.** One day, *I* would like to travel to the Galápagos Islands with my family; *we* could study the giant turtles close up.

EXERCISE B   For each of the following sentences, underline the correct pronoun in parentheses.

EXAMPLE **1.** Slowly, the snake slithered nearer to Michael and (*he*, <u>*him*</u>).

1. Roxanne and (*he, him*) rode horseback this morning.

2. Was it (*he, him*) I saw at the luau?

3. (*They, Them*) were the kindest words the child had ever heard.

4. The guests were not supposed to bring (*they, them*) housewarming gifts.

5. On Sunday, Dad is driving (*hisself, himself*) to Las Cruces.

6. Except for the Bernaths and (*we, us*), everyone has moved away.

7. (*Who, Whom*) did you visit in Luzon last summer?

Continued ☞

Copyright © by Holt, Rinehart and Winston. All rights reserved.

8. Dr. Hernandez was extremely kind to my sister and (*I, me*).

9. (*We, Us*) students wrote the editorial about the plight of our nation's homeless.

10. Besides you and (*he, him*), I have invited Alexis to my bat mitzvah.

11. (*Who, Whom*) is gathering driftwood along the beach?

12. The nursing home gave (*we, us*) volunteers a party.

13. Could it have been (*they, them*) whom you saw in the music store?

14. Mrs. Thomkins assigned the story "A Mother in Manville" to (*we, us*) boys.

15. If it had been Jasper, Dinah, or (*I, me*), we would have been nervous.

16. A salesclerk showed Don and (*I, me*) to the electronics department.

17. The Dobrowskis and (*we, us*) went to see the movie *Anastasia*.

18. The Alvarezes (*theirselves, themselves*) went surfing in Hawaii.

19. The Spanish Club prepared (*we, us*) a special meal of *paella*.

20. (*Who, Whom*) was it at the door?

EXERCISE C   Some of the following sentences contain pronouns that have been used incorrectly. Cross out any incorrect pronoun. Then, on the line provided, write the appropriate pronoun. If a sentence is already correct, write *C*.

EXAMPLE _*themselves*_ **1.** Yes, they did build a computer all by ~~theirselves~~.

_____ **1.** She taught Alfredo and he how to develop film.

_____ **2.** Mike and me are heading down to the lake, Dad.

_____ **3.** Will you go along with Mari and them to the library?

_____ **4.** Between you and I, line dancing is not my specialty.

_____ **5.** Did James Earl Jones really give you and he an autograph?

_____ **6.** There in the middle of center court were us Lancers.

_____ **7.** The first one at the bus stop was him.

_____ **8.** Surely, he will make something of hisself.

_____ **9.** Please show Mrs. Foster and I your new invention.

_____ **10.** Who did she assign the role of Joan of Arc?

Copyright © by Holt, Rinehart and Winston. All rights reserved.

LANGUAGE HANDBOOK 5 USING MODIFIERS

WORKSHEET 1 **Comparison of Modifiers** (Rules 5 a, b)

EXERCISE A   For each of the following modifiers, write the comparative and superlative forms.

EXAMPLE	COMPARATIVE	SUPERLATIVE
open	1. _____more open_____	_____most open_____

fierce	1. _____	_____
cautiously	2. _____	_____
wide	3. _____	_____
confidently	4. _____	_____
shy	5. _____	_____
clearly	6. _____	_____
alone	7. _____	_____
joyfully	8. _____	_____
vain	9. _____	_____
dangerous	10. _____	_____

EXERCISE B   On the line provided, identify the degree of comparison of the italicized modifiers in each of the following sentences. Write *POS* for positive degree, *COMP* for comparative degree, and *SUPER* for superlative degree. Then, tell how many things are being compared (*0, 2,* or *more than 2*).

EXAMPLE   _SUPER, more than 2_   **1.** That's the *best* one I've seen.

_____ **1.** Which of these engines runs *most efficiently*?

_____ **2.** Some of the fiction I've been reading is even *stranger* than real life.

_____ **3.** Of all our spelling words, that one is the *hardest* for me.

_____ **4.** Alaska is the *largest* state in the Union.

_____ **5.** Do the storms near Cape Horn or those near Cape of Good Hope blow *more violently*?

_____ **6.** That was the *foggiest* night in my memory.

_____ **7.** Musicians with sticks *loudly* beat the African drums.

_____ **8.** You should brush your teeth *more frequently* than you do now.

_____ **9.** Stay *safe*!

_____ **10.** There were many contestants, but only one would run the *fastest*.

Copyright © by Holt, Rinehart and Winston. All rights reserved.

LANGUAGE HANDBOOK **5** USING MODIFIERS

WORKSHEET 2 | Comparison of Modifiers (Rules 5 a, b)

EXERCISE A For each of the following modifiers, write the comparative and superlative forms.

EXAMPLE		COMPARATIVE	SUPERLATIVE
much	**1.**	*more*	*most*
good	**1.**	_____	_____
many	**2.**	_____	_____
little	**3.**	_____	_____
well	**4.**	_____	_____
bad	**5.**	_____	_____

EXERCISE B On the line provided, identify the degree of comparison of the italicized modifiers in each of the following sentences. Write *POS* for positive degree, *COMP* for comparative degree, and *SUPER* for superlative degree. Then, tell how many things are being compared (*0, 2,* or *more than 2*).

EXAMPLES	
_____*POS, 0*_____	**1.** Hey, that's not a *bad* idea!
_____*COM, 2*_____	**2.** You'll study *better* with fewer distractions.
*SUPER, more than 2*	**3.** Tiger Woods may be the *best* golfer of his generation.

_____ **1.** Many of the *best* rugs in the world are handmade in the Middle East.

_____ **2.** Somehow, the big dog eats *less* than the little one.

_____ **3.** Whoever negotiates *best* wins.

_____ **4.** Who said, "What a *good* boy am I"?

_____ **5.** There is *more* rain this year than last year.

_____ **6.** The manager felt *bad* about the mistake and gave us our lunch free.

_____ **7.** Over time, which of the three printers will cost *least*?

_____ **8.** Which of these five options seems *best* to you?

_____ **9.** Please ask for directions to the Zocalo; you speak *better* Spanish than I.

_____ **10.** Which air conditioner uses the *least* amount of electricity?

Copyright © by Holt, Rinehart and Winston. All rights reserved.

LANGUAGE HANDBOOK **5** USING MODIFIERS

WORKSHEET 3 Choosing Adverbs or Adjectives (Rules 5 a, c, d)

EXERCISE A   In each of the following sentences, underline the correct adjective or adverb in parentheses.

> **EXAMPLE 1.** The flight attendants greeted the passengers (*cheerful, <u>cheerfully</u>*).

1. Ray Charles plays the piano (*beautiful, beautifully*), don't you think?
2. Maria, to our surprise, suddenly seemed (*happy, happily*).
3. Mrs. Kincaid spoke (*eloquent, eloquently*) about human rights.
4. The vegetable stew smells absolutely (*delicious, deliciously*).
5. Paying close attention, Yolanda did the work (*skillful, skillfully*).
6. Jonathan felt (*bad, badly*) because he missed the party.
7. Earline read the recipe (*careful, carefully*) before she began making the tacos.
8. The parachutist floated (*gentle, gently*) down to earth.
9. Theo opened the door (*cautious, cautiously*).
10. Mr. Young Bear paid (*close, closely*) attention to the speaker.

EXERCISE B   In each of the following sentences, underline the correct word in parentheses.

> **EXAMPLE 1.** The group members worked (*good, <u>well</u>*) together.

1. Those totem poles were certainly carved and painted (*good, well*).
2. Jacy drives (*good, well*) for a beginner.
3. From your description, that movie certainly sounds (*good, well*).
4. Atietie, my pal from Nigeria, speaks English very (*good, well*).
5. The dancers performed the routine (*good, well*).
6. Michael feels (*good, well*) about his progress.
7. In the darkness of the cave, they couldn't see very (*good, well*).
8. Everything you do, Iola, you do (*good, well*).
9. Aunt Aretha is recovering quite (*good, well*), the doctors say.
10. A cool shower seems especially (*good, well*) at the end of a hot day.

Copyright © by Holt, Rinehart and Winston. All rights reserved.

WORKSHEET 4 | Choosing Correct Modifiers (Rules 5 b, e, f)

EXERCISE For each of the following sentences, underline the correct answer in parentheses.

> **EXAMPLE** **1.** Don't tell (*no one, anyone*) about the party yet.

1. Your portfolio is (*more neater, neater*) than those of the other students.

2. Few military attacks have been planned with (*more, most*) care than the D-day landings in Normandy.

3. There isn't (*anything, nothing*) on this map to indicate the boundaries of the former Yugoslavia.

4. Hardly (*no one, anyone*) in our class knew that Sandra Cisneros lives in San Antonio.

5. Wow! Out of the whole club, you sold (*the most, more*) tickets.

6. Isn't the Nile the (*most longest, longest*) river in the world?

7. Either backpack is acceptable, but this one is (*less, the least*) expensive.

8. I don't know much about baking, (*either, neither*); I follow the directions on the box.

9. Oh! That is the (*most beautifulest, most beautiful*) song in the world!

10. Of the two in-line skaters, Joelle is (*steadiest, steadier*) on her feet.

11. Unfortunately, the young emperor Nero wasn't prepared for (*any, scarcely any*) of the burdens of leadership.

12. Until recently, these lizards couldn't be found (*nowhere, anywhere*) in North America.

13. This is the sentence that makes the paragraph (*less clear, less clearer*).

14. Which of these four decisions was made (*more responsibly, most responsibly*)?

15. Yikes! The pan is (*more hotter, hotter*) than the stove!

16. You (*can, can't*) take no books into the testing area.

17. Which of these planets is (*closer, closest*) to Earth, Mars or Venus?

18. Don't (*never, ever*) say you can't do something until you've tried.

19. Few countries can provide (*more better, better*) places to ski than Switzerland.

20. All of the ponies seemed timid, but the pinto approached us (*less timidly, least timidly*).

21. Of the three boys, Eric is (*the most kindest, kindest*).

22. Is it true that the Taylors don't watch (*any, no*) TV?

23. Traditionally, the Chinese eat (*less, least*) meat than Americans do.

24. Stratus clouds are one of the (*lowest, most lowest*)-hanging kinds of clouds.

25. Of the world's languages, which is (*more, most*) widely used?

Copyright © by Holt, Rinehart and Winston. All rights reserved.

LANGUAGE HANDBOOK 5 USING MODIFIERS

WORKSHEET 5 Dangling and Misplaced Modifiers (Rule 5 g)

EXERCISE A Each of the following sentences contains a misplaced phrase. Circle each misplaced phrase. Then, use an arrow to indicate where the phrase should be placed.

EXAMPLE **1.** Sonya saw a deer (walking home from school).

1. Eating fish in the river, the couple on the bench saw three otters.

2. On top of the desk, my brother dropped his books.

3. Dogs lunged at the snake barking wildly.

4. Covered with Egyptian hieroglyphics, the scientists were puzzled by the vase.

5. The car caught Daniel's attention painted a deep purple.

EXERCISE B Each of the following sentences contains a dangling phrase. On the line provided, rewrite each sentence so that it is clear. [Hint: You will need to add, delete, or rearrange some words.]

EXAMPLE **1.** Standing on the dock, the ship came into view.
As we were standing on the dock, the ship came into view.

1. Finished with the painting, a new project was begun immediately.

_____

2. Properly prepared, survival is possible in almost any situation.

_____

3. Calling for a vote, a show of hands settled the matter.

_____

4. Cleaning my room, my pet Chihuahua crawled under the bed.

_____

5. Having sighted the whales, a hundred cameras clicked for two full minutes.

_____

Copyright © by Holt, Rinehart and Winston. All rights reserved.

Continued ☞

LANGUAGE HANDBOOK 5   WORKSHEET 5 (continued)

EXERCISE C   Most of the following sentences contain a misplaced or a dangling modifier. First, identify the misplaced or dangling modifier. Then, on the line provided, revise each sentence so that it is clear and correct. If a sentence is already correct, write *C*.

> **EXAMPLE   1.** Saved for a rainy day, the sugar bowl was full of quarters.
> *The sugar bowl was full of quarters that had been saved for a rainy day.*

1. Having completed the first section of the driver's permit test, only ten questions remained. _____

_____

2. Blooming abundantly, their fence was covered with morning glories. _____

_____

3. Derek received high marks from the judges, playing a flawless cornet solo. _____

_____

4. Having been to Egypt, the museum's exhibit was especially interesting to Tina. _____

_____

5. While jogging, they found a watch where someone had dropped it. _____

_____

6. Although tired from hiking, five more miles of trail remained. _____

_____

7. Surprised by the election results, no celebration had been planned. _____

_____

8. I stared up at the clouds waiting in the doorway. _____

_____

9. Before starting research, a topic should be limited. _____

_____

10. When planting a tree, buried cables and water lines must be avoided. _____

_____

Copyright © by Holt, Rinehart and Winston. All rights reserved.

LANGUAGE
HANDBOOK **5** USING MODIFIERS

WORKSHEET 6 | Dangling and Misplaced Modifiers (Rule 5 g)

EXERCISE A   Each of the following sentences contains a misplaced clause. Circle each misplaced clause. Then, draw an arrow to show where the misplaced clause belongs.

   EXAMPLE 1. Bitter winds swept the coast (that blew in from the North).

   1. The owl swooped down on a mouse, which had a two-foot wingspan.

   2. Brightly wrapped boxes lined the hall that had yet to be opened.

   3. Her cabinet had been made in the eighteenth century, which was quite valuable.

   4. The musicians will be signing autographs that played at the concert.

   5. My mother talked to her dog, who was combing her hair.

   6. Australians protect their koalas whose distinctive speech is instantly recognizable.

   7. Helicopters flew over the houses that were used on training missions for pilots.

   8. The load put too much weight on the axle, which was over three thousand pounds.

   9. Dust swirled around the fort that had blown in from the plains.

   10. Flowers sprang up around the cabin that included every color in the rainbow.

EXERCISE B   Most of the following sentences contain a misplaced clause. First, identify the misplaced clause. Then, on the line provided, revise the sentence. If a sentence is correct, write *C*.

   EXAMPLE 1. The golf ball lay in the sand trap that Mr. Lawrence had hit.
   The golf ball that Mr. Lawrence had hit lay in the sand trap.

   1. Angela leaned down and picked up the baby, who had just returned from aerobics class.

   _____

   2. Signs hung on the walls near the water fountain that announced the sale of Girl Scout cookies.

   _____

   3. The car raced around the track, which had recently been refueled at a pit stop.

   _____

   4. Libya borders the Mediterranean Sea, whose capital is Tripoli.

   _____

   5. When they went to the bay to go fishing, the children saw raccoons.

   _____

Copyright © by Holt, Rinehart and Winston. All rights reserved.

NAME _____ CLASS _____ DATE _____

LANGUAGE HANDBOOK 5 USING MODIFIERS

WORKSHEET 7 Correcting Dangling and Misplaced Modifiers (Rule 5 g)

EXERCISE A Each of the following sentences does not make sense because a modifying phrase is in the wrong place. Underline each misplaced phrase. Then, draw an arrow to show where the phrase belongs.

EXAMPLE 1. Marvella served cold milk to the guests <u>in mugs</u>.

1. The explorers hiked all day in the valley wearing rain gear.

2. Mr. Jefferson lectured about bridge construction in the auditorium.

3. Sara could smell her mother's delicious enchiladas in the oven on the porch.

4. Veniece told Shani about Dr. Martin Luther King, Jr.'s life in the library.

5. They built a house for the Sánchez family with three chimneys.

EXERCISE B On the lines provided, rewrite the following sentences by placing the modifying phrases or clauses where they belong.

EXAMPLE 1. With fish from a bucket for their behavior, the animal trainer rewarded the dolphins.
With fish from a bucket, the animal trainer rewarded the dolphins for their behavior.

1. Jaime took the bag to the recycle center with empty aluminum cans.

_____

_____

2. The security guard turned the power off on duty at the Kitami Computer Center.

_____

_____

3. Harriet by her enthusiasm for cycling is often carried away.

_____

_____

4. Murals of Cretan people graced the ancient walls, who lived long ago.

_____

_____

5. We watched the goose fly over the trees whose wing had finally healed.

_____

_____

54 *Language Handbook Worksheets*

Elements of Literature

Copyright © by Holt, Rinehart and Winston. All rights reserved.

LANGUAGE HANDBOOK 5 USING MODIFIERS

| WORKSHEET 8 | Test (Rules 5 a–g)

EXERCISE A For each of the following sentences, underline the appropriate modifier in parentheses.

> **EXAMPLE 1.** Is classical architecture the (*more*, *most*) symmetrical of all styles?

1. Were the Phoenicians or the Romans (*the best, better*) sailors?

2. What is the (*more common, most common*) word in the English language?

3. Do you think the black lacquered furniture of Japan is (*most beautifully, more beautifully*) decorated than Colonial-style furniture from the United States?

4. Lin played her clarinet solo very (*good, well*) in regional competition.

5. "Congratulations, Gina. I read thirty essays, but yours answered the question (*more, most*) intelligently."

6. Vernon's parrot is the (*more mischievous, most mischievous*) of all his pets.

7. Paul liked fly fishing (*more, most*) than still fishing.

8. The aroma in the kitchen from the baked apples smelled (*good, well*).

9. Which is (*less, least*)—three fourths or twelve fifteenths?

10. This translation is the (*most, more*) easily understood of the three.

EXERCISE B For each of the following sentences, underline the modifier that correctly completes the sentence.

> **EXAMPLE 1.** What is the (*tallest, most tallest*) tree in the world?

1. A rectangle is (*more longer, longer*) on one pair of sides than on the other pair.

2. Although the plate looked (*clean, cleanly*), it had not been washed.

3. Is the sloth one of the (*slowest, most slowest*) animals on earth?

4. The mustang remained (*wild, wildly*) for many months.

5. Why do some lights shine (*brighter, more brighter*) than others?

6. That was the (*best, most best*) idea I've heard yet.

7. Jerome's band sounded (*loud, loudly*) to his neighbors.

8. Which was the (*cleverest, most cleverest*) of Benjamin Franklin's inventions?

9. Many people consider this act the (*most important, most importantest*) in civil rights legislation.

10. Don't the Himalayas boast the (*highest, most highest*) peaks in the world?

Continued ☞

Copyright © by Holt, Rinehart and Winston. All rights reserved.

LANGUAGE HANDBOOK 5 **WORKSHEET 8** *(continued)*

EXERCISE C   For each of the following sentences, underline the correct word in parentheses.

> **EXAMPLE 1.** I can't find (*nothing*, *anything*) wrong with this bike.

1. There is (*anything, nothing*) left to do on my homework list.

2. Genghis Khan was not known for taking prisoners alive (*either, neither*).

3. I cannot find the difference between rhythm and beat (*anywhere, nowhere*).

4. She doesn't have (*any, no*) ice skates either.

5. Didn't (*anyone, no one*) tell you how to get to Avenida Juarez?

6. Scarcely (*no one, anyone*) has seen that film yet.

7. Amazingly, the magician didn't break (*any, none*) of the glasses.

8. We are not (*anywhere, nowhere*) near a phone right now.

9. Haven't you (*ever, never*) seen a professional stage play?

10. He went to three stores, but he couldn't find (*none, one*) of those shirts.

EXERCISE D   Most of the following sentences contain misplaced or dangling phrases or clauses. Identify each misplaced or dangling modifier. Then, on the line provided, revise each sentence so that it is clear and correct. If a sentence is correct, write *C*.

> **EXAMPLE 1.** Totally lost in Mexico City, no one had a map.
> *Totally lost in Mexico City, we needed a map.*

1. The poem was written by James Weldon Johnson that we read today._____

_____

2. He studied the one-celled organism in pond water squinting through the lens of the microscope._____

_____

3. Many famous places can be seen, driving down Paseo de la Reforma._____

_____

4. Painted a deep shade of green, the Studebaker was admired by many car buffs. _____

_____

5. Hiding behind the sofa, Mom opened the door while we waited with her birthday presents._____

_____

Copyright © by Holt, Rinehart and Winston. All rights reserved.

LANGUAGE HANDBOOK **6** PHRASES

| WORKSHEET 1 | **Identifying Prepositional Phrases (Rules 6 a, b)**

EXERCISE A   Underline each prepositional phrase in the following sentences.

> **EXAMPLES 1.** <u>Under certain conditions</u>, scientists can tell what happens <u>during sleep</u>.
>
> **2.** A person changes body position about a dozen times <u>during an average night</u> <u>of sleep</u>.

1. In the laboratory, subjects have electrodes attached to their heads.

2. Electrodes transmit signals from the brain.

3. These signals, called brain waves, are recorded on a graph.

4. After many experiments, scientists can now identify the shapes of certain brain waves.

5. During deep sleep, brain waves of the subjects are large and very slow.

6. Brain waves of dreaming subjects, however, are similar to those of awake persons.

7. The brain waves form rapid, small, irregular patterns on the graph.

8. In addition, the eyes of the dreamers move rapidly under closed eyelids.

9. Subjects awakened during dreaming sleep remember their dreams approximately eighty percent of the time.

10. Dreaming sleep also occurs in cats, dogs, and elephants, and even in some reptiles.

EXERCISE B   Underline each prepositional phrase in the following sentences.

> **EXAMPLE 1.** <u>Across Ortega Bay</u>, cottages <u>of whitewashed stone</u> <u>from the local stone quarry</u> line the road <u>to the pier</u>.

1. The residents of the island eagerly await the arrival of the boat from the mainland.

2. Every morning, at the stroke of ten, the boat from the mainland docks there.

3. The boat brings mail and supplies to the residents of the island.

4. Most of the passengers on the boat are tourists.

5. With skill and determination, the captain of the boat, Consuelo Padilla, brings her vessel safely to port.

6. Captain Padilla received her earliest training from her father.

7. Her father had worked on many boats of all sizes.

8. For many years, he saved part of his salary to buy this boat.

9. Before he retired, the first Captain Padilla piloted this boat for twenty years.

10. He is proud of his daughter who has followed in his footsteps.

Copyright © by Holt, Rinehart and Winston. All rights reserved.

LANGUAGE HANDBOOK **6** **PHRASES**

WORKSHEET 2 | **Identifying Adjective Phrases (Rule 6 c)**

EXERCISE A   Underline each adjective phrase in the following sentences. Then, draw an arrow from the phrase to the noun or pronoun it modifies.

> **EXAMPLE** **1.** The sound <u>of falling rain</u> can be very soothing.

1. Who is the woman in the blue coat?

2. The family across the street just adopted two Persian cats.

3. Latrice composes music for her favorite poems.

4. That old-fashioned house with the wide porch is being painted.

5. The Perezes proudly served plantains from their own garden.

6. Books about Anasazi culture covered her desk.

7. Is that mahogany table in the hall too large?

8. A smaller one with a convenient drawer would be more suitable.

9. Boxes of every shape and size filled the room.

10. Patricia won tickets to the Super Bowl game.

EXERCISE B   Complete each of the following sentences by writing an appropriate adjective phrase on the line provided.

> **EXAMPLE** **1.** The McBean family moved into a new house _____*near the glen*_____.

1. In the safe was a black box _____.

2. A photographer _____ took pictures of the Kwanzaa celebration.

3. Last week we attended the game _____.

4. The historic agreement _____ still exists today.

5. Some _____ are members of that club.

6. This autographed picture _____ belongs to Aunt Coretta.

7. Mr. Poiter has just returned from a trip _____.

8. Everyone _____ has been vaccinated.

9. An apartment _____ is no place to keep a large dog.

10. Finally, Chim selected three _____.

Copyright © by Holt, Rinehart and Winston. All rights reserved.

Elements of Literature

LANGUAGE HANDBOOK	**6**	PHRASES

WORKSHEET 3	Identifying Adjective and Adverb Phrases (Rules 6 c, d)

EXERCISE A   Underline each adverb phrase in the following sentences. Then, draw an arrow from the phrase to the word or words it modifies.

> **EXAMPLE 1.** Garnetta Jordan, a town council member, called <u>at our house</u>.

1. Mrs. Jordan was campaigning for a third term.

2. She was accompanied by a television crew and radio announcers.

3. My father and mother have known the councilor for many years.

4. The camera operators shone bright lights on our faces.

5. Meanwhile, Mrs. Jordan discussed some issues with my parents.

6. She left late in the afternoon.

7. We all were dazed by this sudden visit, and we were relieved by her departure.

8. The interview was shown on the evening news.

9. Several friends telephoned my parents after the newscast.

10. During dinner my parents and I discussed some issues.

EXERCISE B   Underline each prepositional phrase in the following sentences. Then, on the line provided, write *ADJ* if the phrase is an adjective phrase or *ADV* if it is an adverb phrase.

> **EXAMPLE** _ADV_ **1.** The writer Lina Mao Wall was born <u>in Cambodia</u>.

_____ **1.** Kitty watched the Rose Bowl parade from the bleachers.

_____ **2.** Latwanda read a book about Chief Joseph.

_____ **3.** The chef made a large salad of romaine lettuce, olives, jalapeño peppers, tomatoes, and feta cheese.

_____ **4.** The Greek god Zeus ruled Olympus with wisdom and power.

_____ **5.** Mr. Sanford directed the play during Mrs. Knight's absence.

_____ **6.** The whole family went to the homecoming game.

_____ **7.** They didn't leave until one o'clock.

_____ **8.** The artist has painted a beautiful picture of the pagoda.

_____ **9.** Mayor Shapiro always greets us with a big smile.

_____ **10.** The National Air and Space Museum has become very popular with tourists, students, and scientists.

Copyright © by Holt, Rinehart and Winston. All rights reserved.

WORKSHEET 4 | **Identifying Prepositional Phrases (Rules 6 a–d)**

EXERCISE A   Underline each prepositional phrase in the following sentences.

> EXAMPLE **1.** Most students picture themselves <u>with interesting jobs in exciting fields</u>.

1. Some people want jobs that take them outside the realm of ordinary experience.

2. Grace Wiley had one of those careers.

3. Wiley was a well-known herpetologist, an expert on snakes.

4. She had one of the world's largest collections of snakes.

5. She kept her snakes in the barn behind her house.

6. She had many different kinds of snakes, which she would often show to tourists.

7. Inside the barn were cages with vipers, rattlesnakes, kraits, and cobras.

8. In many cultures, people have at the same time feared and revered snakes.

9. One of the most fascinating kinds of snakes is the cobra.

10. Cobras are very large snakes that come from Asia or Africa.

11. Around a cobra's neck is a loose fold of skin.

12. This fold of skin expands into a hood when the cobra becomes excited.

13. Wiley studied the cobras in her collection and learned about their habits.

14. She learned that during an attack the cobra rears straight upward.

15. A hand held above the head of the standing cobra is outside the cobra's range.

16. Some cobras deliver venom through bites in their victims' skin, and others spit poison into the eyes of their victims.

17. Wiley must not have been afraid of her cobras.

18. She would often let a cobra strike the flattened palm of one of her hands.

19. Unfortunately, Wiley was bitten by one of her cobras when she was posing for a publicity photograph.

20. Although she kept antivenom serum for emergencies, the only vial broke, and Wiley died as a result of the bite.

Copyright © by Holt, Rinehart and Winston. All rights reserved.

Continued ☞

EXERCISE B   Underline each prepositional phrase in the following sentences. Then, draw an arrow from the phrase to the word it modifies.

> EXAMPLE 1. The stories <u>from ancient cultures</u> are fascinating.

1. Many ancient peoples had stories about the sky.

2. In one African folk tale, the god Obatala descended from the sky on a golden chain.

3. Hanging from the chain, he poured sand into the sea below him.

4. The Yoruba legend said Obatala created dry land in this manner.

5. Early Scandinavians looked with concern at the universe.

6. One ancient story tells a tale of a mighty ash tree.

7. All of the universe is supported by this tree.

8. Its three great roots reach into the regions of the gods, of the giants, and of darkness and cold.

9. A serpent with a great hunger gnaws continuously at the tree's roots.

10. One day the tree may fall, and the universe may crash onto the heads of people.

EXERCISE C   Underline each prepositional phrase in the following sentences. Above each phrase, write *ADJ* if it is an adjective phrase or *ADV* if it is an adverb phrase.

>   ADJ   ADJ   ADJ
> EXAMPLE 1. Everyone <u>in camp</u> awaited the return <u>of Young Bear</u> <u>from his mission</u>.

1. The Dakota scout knew the trail along the river.

2. The scout rode swiftly to camp and gave his report.

3. The commander sent messengers to all the neighboring camps.

4. The enemy proceeded cautiously through the mountain passes and approached the Dakota settlements on the plains.

5. The enemy's plan of attack was foiled by the combined forces of the Dakotas.

Copyright © by Holt, Rinehart and Winston. All rights reserved.

LANGUAGE HANDBOOK **6** **PHRASES**

WORKSHEET 5 Identifying Participles and Participial Phrases (Rules 6 e, f)

EXERCISE A Underline the past participle or past participial phrase in each of the following sentences. Then, circle the word or words that it modifies.

> **EXAMPLE 1.** <u>Taken at the party</u>, this (photograph) will be a gift for our guests.

1. An antelope of delicate blown glass stands in the window.

2. In his own lifetime, Thomas Alva Edison would become an inventor celebrated the world over.

3. White ribbons top the brightly wrapped present.

4. Pearls found in the waters off Bahrain, an island in the Persian Gulf, can be quite valuable.

5. Is the scheduled train to Berlin on time?

6. Hidden for centuries, a vein of gold awaits discovery.

7. Many men in Algeria wear a burnoose, a long, hooded cloak.

8. Behind the door hangs his new suit, fitted especially for him by the best tailor in town.

9. Please put the vase of cut flowers on the dinner table.

10. By now, the proposal, completed in time for the conference, should be sitting on her desk.

EXERCISE B Underline the present participle or present participial phrase in each of the following sentences. Then, draw an arrow from each participle or participial phrase to the noun it modifies.

> **EXAMPLE 1.** The picture <u>hanging above the sofa</u> is a print of a painting by Pablo Picasso.

1. Laying aside her notes, Tamisha improvised her speech about the importance of recycling.

2. Rosalia, hoping to see her friend from the old neighborhood, watched the windows of the bus anxiously.

3. Carrying his bucket of paint, Ossie climbed down the ladder.

4. Telling everyone about the soccer match, Keanu delayed the club meeting for nearly an hour.

5. The baby sitter tried to comfort the sobbing toddler.

Copyright © by Holt, Rinehart and Winston. All rights reserved.

Elements of Literature

LANGUAGE HANDBOOK 6 PHRASES

WORKSHEET 6

Identifying Gerunds and Gerund Phrases (Rules 6 g, h)

EXERCISE A Underline each gerund in the following sentences.

> **EXAMPLE 1.** Is <u>acting</u> easy for you, Ms. Winfrey?

1. The Pomo Indians were so good at weaving that some of their baskets could hold water.

2. Can just talking solve a problem?

3. Why don't you give diving a try?

4. Possibly the most important occupation in the world is farming.

5. Luis had just returned from sailing and had not yet eaten lunch.

6. Next on our agenda comes shopping for Tracy and John's wedding present.

7. She is focused on swimming.

8. Leading the participants, the host of the games announced that wrestling was to begin.

9. Students arriving late will not be admitted during testing.

10. Give your handwriting a little more attention this year.

EXERCISE B Underline each gerund or gerund phrase in the following sentences. On the line provided, write how the gerund is used in the sentence. Use the following abbreviations: Write *S* for subject, *DO* for direct object, *OP* for object of a preposition, or *PN* for predicate nominative.

> **EXAMPLE** ___DO___ **1.** Wow! Who taught you <u>signing</u>?

_____ 1. Winning at all costs can be very expensive.

_____ 2. Robert really likes baking bread and rolls.

_____ 3. Mr. Rodriquez is through with traveling on business so much.

_____ 4. Sachi's hobby has always been collecting baseball cards.

_____ 5. Finding the last item on the scavenger hunt took us almost an hour.

_____ 6. Stand back! The baby loves splashing in the bath.

_____ 7. Driving a car is a serious responsibility and a task requiring all your attention.

_____ 8. The discussion centered around designing a bicycle.

_____ 9. Marissa's first love is playing the piano.

_____ 10. Did you learn sand painting from a Pueblo teacher?

Copyright © by Holt, Rinehart and Winston. All rights reserved.

LANGUAGE HANDBOOK 6 PHRASES

| WORKSHEET 7 | **Identifying Infinitives and Infinitive Phrases (Rules 6 i, j)** |

EXERCISE A   Underline the infinitive or infinitive phrase in each of the following sentences.

> EXAMPLE **1.** One way <u>to learn effectively</u> is by asking good questions.

1. To save a file on this computer, press F9.

2. To have everything is not possible, so you must make choices.

3. Antonio Novello was the first Hispanic to become surgeon general of the United States.

4. It's good to hear your voice for the first time since your trip to Miami.

5. My little brother wants to go everywhere with me.

6. We still have much to learn about outer space.

7. I just called to say hello to my best friend.

8. You'll be the first to know if I get a part in the class play.

9. The movers put a box there to prop the door open.

10. Columbus's plan was to discover a new route to the East.

EXERCISE B   Underline each infinitive or infinitive phase in the following sentences. Then, on the line provided, write how the infinitive or infinitive phrase is used in the sentence. Use the following abbreviations: Write *N* for noun, *ADJ* for adjective, or *ADV* for adverb.

> EXAMPLE __ADV__ **1.** Nothing was left <u>to say</u>.

_____ **1.** To complete every item is not always important on some tests.

_____ **2.** A sight to see during the Chinese New Year is people dressing as dragons.

_____ **3.** They laughed to see the monkey's antics.

_____ **4.** Remember to call us when you get there.

_____ **5.** The first one in will be the last to leave.

_____ **6.** Sending e-mail can be easy to do.

_____ **7.** To ensure delivery of your letters, always use complete ZIP Codes.

_____ **8.** The goal for that Saturday was to make pumpkin bread from scratch.

_____ **9.** There will be much to explore at the Maya ruins in Chichén Itzá.

_____ **10.** Listen carefully to avoid any misunderstanding.

Continued ☞

Copyright © by Holt, Rinehart and Winston. All rights reserved.

EXERCISE C Underline each infinitive or infinitive phrase in the following sentences. On the line provided, write how each infinitive or infinitive phrase is used. Use the following abbreviations: Write *S* for subject, *DO* for direct object, or *PN* for predicate nominative.

EXAMPLE _DO_ **1.** Her company planned <u>to provide chairs for the convention</u>.

_____ **1.** To forgive is not always easy but is always worthwhile.

_____ **2.** That morning in Brussels, it started to snow, and it snowed all day.

_____ **3.** Is the object of the game to capture all the pieces?

_____ **4.** We like to write everything as well as we can.

_____ **5.** His greatest satisfaction was to serve his country.

EXERCISE D Underline each infinitive or infinitive phrase in the following sentences. Then, on the line provided, write how the infinitive or infinitive phrase is used in the sentence. Use the following abbreviations: *N* for noun, *ADJ* for adjective, or *ADV* for adverb.

EXAMPLE _N_ **1.** I promised <u>to return Mrs. Johnson's books in two weeks</u>.

_____ **1.** Our final assignment was to write a report on a subject that interested us.

_____ **2.** To choose a topic was very hard because I am interested in many things.

_____ **3.** I talked with my parents to see what they thought about some topics.

_____ **4.** When I had narrowed the topics to five, it was time to go to the library.

_____ **5.** With the help of Ms. Johnson, the librarian, I learned to use the new online catalog.

_____ **6.** Three of my topics had few sources, so my choices were easy to narrow.

_____ **7.** To see which topic had the best information, I looked at the remaining sources.

_____ **8.** Wow! On the topic of whales, there were four books and nine articles to read.

_____ **9.** I chose one book and three articles and took them to Ms. Johnson to check out.

_____ **10.** I learned enough to be the class expert on whales while I was working on my report.

Copyright © by Holt, Rinehart and Winston. All rights reserved.

WORKSHEET 8 | **Identifying Appositives and Appositive Phrases
(Rules 6 k, l)**

EXERCISE A   Underline each appositive or appositive phrase in the following
sentences.

> **EXAMPLE 1.** The garment, <u>a traditional Indian sari</u>, was wrapped
> carefully around her body.

1. Number 53, a favorite with the crowd, is expected to break the record this game.

2. From the balcony, I looked out at the familiar sights—rooftops, treetops, and the houses of my old neighborhood.

3. The soloist bowed and picked up his instrument, a violin.

4. Ask Mr. Fulton, the man in the black beret over there, about the entrance fee.

5. My mother, a teacher at our school, also coaches the debate team.

6. Didn't Alexander, our school's best sprinter, win an award in track?

7. The trip, my first outside our home state, lasted for two weeks.

8. I studied the lines on his face, a map of every emotion felt in his seventy years.

9. These masks, fine examples of African art, strongly influenced Pablo Picasso.

10. These colors—green, white, and red—are the colors of the Mexican flag.

EXERCISE B   Underline each appositive or appositive phrase in the following
sentences. Then, on the line provided, write the word or words that the appositive or
appositive phrase identifies or explains.

> **EXAMPLE** _novel_ **1.** Have you read Gary Paulsen's novel _Hatchet_ yet?

_____ 1. The story "Oni and the Great Bird" is a Yoruban tale.

_____ 2. In the suitcase were souvenirs from a lifetime—ticket stubs, letters, photographs, and many other items.

_____ 3. Now, let us welcome Carl Lewis, a nine-time Olympic gold medal winner!

_____ 4. A row of mirrors greeted visitors on their way through the exhibit, the last one in the museum.

_____ 5. Some of the students carried small computers, the latest craze among middle schoolers.

Copyright © by Holt, Rinehart and Winston. All rights reserved.

Elements of Literature

WORKSHEET 9 **Test (Rules 6 a–l)**

EXERCISE A   Underline each prepositional phrase. Then, circle the word or words that the phrase modifies.

EXAMPLE 1. (Take) me to the art museum, please.

1. Tiny streams of lava still flowed from the Kilauea volcano.

2. When spring came, Viking ships attacked from the north.

3. The path near the top of the cliff was steep and rocky.

4. Twenty Arabian horses and their riders participated in the parade.

5. Is algebra easy for you?

6. This African house was made of sun-dried mud.

7. Do come into the house from the cold.

8. In the garden grew bright tulips and yellow daffodils.

9. Have you ever written to the author Amy Tan?

10. The area above the tree line is almost uninhabited.

EXERCISE B   Underline the participle or participial phrase in each of the following sentences. Then, on the line provided, write the word that the participle or participial phrase modifies.

EXAMPLE _cup_ 1. The cup, fabled for its healing powers, eluded archaeologists.

_____ 1. Their yard had a freshly painted fence.

_____ 2. You'll need more than a winning smile to compete in the talent show.

_____ 3. Skilled workers repaired the cables of the bridge.

_____ 4. Look! There's a bear heading for the trout stream.

_____ 5. Some of the great sailing ships appeared in the harbor that day.

_____ 6. Now, where did I leave my tinted glasses?

_____ 7. Who painted that picture of a boy wearing a blue suit?

_____ 8. In the Philippines, heavily decorated vehicles, or *jeepneys*, are used as taxis.

_____ 9. At camp, we read by the glow of lanterns flickering in the breeze.

_____ 10. The bottle, carried by sea currents to this beach, came from Mexico.

Continued ☞

Copyright © by Holt, Rinehart and Winston. All rights reserved.

EXERCISE C   Underline each gerund or gerund phrase in the following sentences. Then, on the line provided, write how the gerund or gerund phrase is being used. Use the following abbreviations: Write *S* for subject, *DO* for direct object, *OP* for object of a preposition, or *PN* for predicate nominative. A sentence may have more than one gerund or gerund phrase.

EXAMPLE ___*S*___ **1.** <u>Grazing</u> takes up most of a wild horse's day.

_____ **1.** Learning Vietnamese requires concentration.

_____ **2.** We really enjoyed picnicking in the park.

_____ **3.** Mother Teresa was concerned with helping the poor.

_____ **4.** Does he devote much of his leisure time to exercising?

_____ **5.** The blast dulled our hearing for some time.

_____ **6.** Building the Great Wall of China took centuries.

_____ **7.** One of Mr. Hena's hobbies is sewing.

_____ **8.** Please start washing the dishes, Ted.

_____ **9.** The ticking of the clock broke the silence.

_____ **10.** The first step in writing an essay is planning.

EXERCISE D   Underline the infinitive or infinitive phrase in each of the following sentences. On the line provided, write *N* if the phrase is used as a noun, *ADJ* if it is used as an adjective, or *ADV* if it is used as an adverb.

EXAMPLE ___*ADV*___ **1.** You are so kind <u>to think of us</u>!

_____ **1.** The play starts at 7:00, and we don't want to arrive late.

_____ **2.** You're clever to have figured that out.

_____ **3.** To cool off, the elephants flapped their ears.

_____ **4.** Put the blankets out to air before storing them.

_____ **5.** To fly with the U.S. Navy Blue Angels is her dream.

_____ **6.** She's just the person to help us with the horses.

_____ **7.** My mom promised to drive to the Museum of International Folk Art.

_____ **8.** They are looking for someone to lead the team.

_____ **9.** Who wasn't surprised to see the amount of damage to the *Titanic*?

_____ **10.** A scout rode ahead to blaze a trail for the wagon train.

Continued ☞

Copyright © by Holt, Rinehart and Winston. All rights reserved.

EXERCISE E   Underline the appositive or appositive phrase in each of the following sentences. On the line provided, write the word or words that the appositive or appositive phrase identifies or explains.

EXAMPLE ___*Eric*___ **1.** Did Eric the Red have a last name?

_____ **1.** His dog, a Mexican Chihuahua, was both fierce and fearless.

_____ **2.** A crowd gathered around the antique car, a Model T.

_____ **3.** This answer should have been the third choice, "the Revolutionary War."

_____ **4.** How did he learn about work and friendship from the Irish setter Big Red?

_____ **5.** The Sydney Opera House, an amazing feat of architecture, overlooks the harbor.

_____ **6.** Station managers hired my uncle, Lucas Davis, to work at the ticket counter.

_____ **7.** Listen to her aunt, a Cherokee with hundreds of stories to tell.

_____ **8.** Lynda sent some photos to her stepsister Carol.

_____ **9.** In Hawaii, the luau, an outdoor feast and celebration, is quite popular with tourists.

_____ **10.** We watched the P-38, one of the great fighter planes, as it taxied past us and took off.

Copyright © by Holt, Rinehart and Winston. All rights reserved.

LANGUAGE
HANDBOOK **7** CLAUSES

WORKSHEET 1 | **Identifying Independent Clauses and Subordinate Clauses (Rules 7 a–c)**

EXERCISE A   Identify each of the following word groups. On the line provided, write *I* for an independent clause and *S* for a subordinate clause.

EXAMPLE ___*S*___ **1.** whom the coach chose

_____ **1.** who was wearing red sunglasses at the mall yesterday

_____ **2.** since the Civil War ended

_____ **3.** if reservations are desired and you wish to be seated early

_____ **4.** the locomotive built up steam

_____ **5.** that contributions to science helped create today's world

_____ **6.** before people realized that the earth revolves around the sun

_____ **7.** while we were playing a soccer game

_____ **8.** he must be working in the garage

_____ **9.** that flock of birds flew to their nests

_____ **10.** which she decides to do

EXERCISE B   On the line provided, add an independent clause to each of the following subordinate clauses to make a clear and complete sentence.

EXAMPLE **1.** when the corn was waist high

*When the corn was waist high, we hoed between the rows every day.*

1. because the temperature was so high

_____

2. whomever they elect

_____

3. although they had visited their relatives in Mexico before

_____

4. whose name, even after hundreds of years, is still recognized and respected

_____

5. when, to our surprise, a gerbil scampered out from under the sofa

_____

Copyright © by Holt, Rinehart and Winston. All rights reserved.

LANGUAGE HANDBOOK **7** CLAUSES

WORSHEET 2 | **Identifying and Using Adjective Clauses (Rule 7 d)**

EXERCISE A   Underline the adjective clause in each of the following sentences. Then, circle the relative pronoun in each clause. On the line provided, write the word or words to which the relative pronoun refers.

EXAMPLE ___one___ **1.** She's the one (whose) cat likes our dog.

_____ **1.** Can anyone name the person who created a vaccine for polio?

_____ **2.** The next story was by an author whose work she was already reading.

_____ **3.** Is that the company that installed the computers?

_____ **4.** All thoroughbred horses, which include most racehorses, are descendants of three Arabian stallions.

_____ **5.** The man with whom the mayor spoke was the ambassador to Mexico.

_____ **6.** Stones that had been quarried nearby lined the fireplace walls.

_____ **7.** Australia's Great Barrier Reef, which attracts many swimmers, also attracts skin divers.

_____ **8.** This poem was written by Shel Silverstein, a poet who has a wonderful sense of humor.

_____ **9.** The scientist to whom our teacher referred was George Washington Carver.

_____ **10.** Romare Bearden, whose collages reflect the lives of African Americans, studied in Paris at the Sorbonne.

EXERCISE B   Each of the following items is a noun modified by an adjective or an adjective phrase. On the lines provided, revise each item to make it a noun modified by an adjective clause.

EXAMPLE **1.** the boy with the new shoes _the boy whose shoes are new_

1. the gray horse _____

2. the computers at our school _____

3. the first-string basketball players _____

4. the dog with the bone _____

5. the minivan in the garage _____

Copyright © by Holt, Rinehart and Winston. All rights reserved.

Continued ☞

LANGUAGE HANDBOOK 7 WORKSHEET 2 *(continued)*

EXERCISE C   On the line provided, add an independent clause to each of the following adjective clauses to make a clear and complete sentence. Then, circle the relative pronoun.

EXAMPLE **1.** that we saw under the microscope

Hydras were the creatures (that) we saw under the microscope.

1. whose paintings are valued at millions of dollars

_____

2. whom Mom always calls Jake

_____

3. who had always liked horses

_____

4. which was no surprise to any of us

_____

5. that hung from the ceiling

_____

6. whom we have known for years

_____

7. which is a story told in many lands

_____

8. whose cooking delights our whole family

_____

9. who raises champion sheep

_____

10. that was in the trunk of the car

_____

Copyright © by Holt, Rinehart and Winston. All rights reserved.

LANGUAGE
HANDBOOK **7** CLAUSES

WORKSHEET 3 Identifying Adverb Clauses (Rule 7 e)

EXERCISE A   Underline the adverb clause in each of the following sentences. On the line provided, write the subordinating conjunction that begins the clause.

EXAMPLE _as soon as_ **1.** Let me know <u>as soon as the mail arrives</u>.

_____ **1.** The engine runs much more smoothly after it has a tune-up.

_____ **2.** When the crane arrives, it will hoist the sign into place.

_____ **3.** Excalibur would remain in the stone until the future king drew it out.

_____ **4.** Since we celebrated Hanukkah, she has been making plans for the next holiday.

_____ **5.** Some plants will not bear fruit unless they experience a hard freeze.

_____ **6.** You're really playing better this season than you did last season.

_____ **7.** I must have picked up the phone just as you finished dialing.

_____ **8.** Wind causes erosion because it blows topsoil away.

_____ **9.** He looked as though he didn't understand a single word.

_____ **10.** If you travel south on the Pan American Highway from Arizona or Texas, you can reach seventeen Latin American countries.

EXERCISE B   Underline the adverb clause in each of the following sentences. On the line provided, write whether the clause answers *how, when, where, why, to what extent,* or *under what conditions.*

EXAMPLE ____when____ **1.** Turn down the heat <u>when the soup boils</u>.

_____ **1.** She goes mountain biking as often as she can.

_____ **2.** While the photographers took pictures, reporters interviewed the winner.

_____ **3.** Porpoises gather in cool, coastal waters wherever food is plentiful.

_____ **4.** Because their roots are deep, these plants survived the drought.

_____ **5.** While I have both CDs and records, I prefer the sound quality of the CDs.

_____ **6.** The Great Pyramid of Egypt looked as if it had been cut from one large, white stone.

_____ **7.** I work at my dad's printing shop as much as my schedule permits.

_____ **8.** Officials make regular inspections so that safety standards will be met.

_____ **9.** Before calculators became widely available, people used adding machines.

_____ **10.** If you want to get to Honduras from Mexico by land, you must travel through Guatemala.

Copyright © by Holt, Rinehart and Winston. All rights reserved.

LANGUAGE
HANDBOOK **7** **CLAUSES**

WORKSHEET 4 **Identifying Noun Clauses** (Rule 7 f)

EXERCISE A   Underline the noun clause in each of the following sentences.

> **EXAMPLE 1.** The treasure belongs to <u>whoever finds it</u>.

1. Not every school accepts whoever applies.
2. That the equator runs through Kenya is evident from the map.
3. Paul doesn't know where the scissors are.
4. Whatever you decide will be fine with us.
5. The lock will belong to whoever knows the combination.
6. Who told you that José Greco is one of the world's best flamenco dancers?
7. Save that twenty dollars for when you really need it.
8. In five minutes, I will read whoever is sitting on the rug a story.
9. College is what I am planning after I graduate from high school.
10. From what the newspapers say, the debate will continue for some time.

EXERCISE B   Underline the noun clause in each of the following sentences. On the line provided, write how the clause is used in the sentence. Use the following abbreviations: Write *S* for subject, *IO* for indirect object, *DO* for direct object, *PN* for predicate nominative, or *OP* for object of a preposition.

> **EXAMPLE** __*DO*__ **1.** Know <u>what you want</u> before you place your order.

_____ 1. Maria was whom they chose for class president.

_____ 2. What happened at the Olympics surprised many sports fans.

_____ 3. Would you show me how you made that?

_____ 4. That the longbow was an effective weapon soon became obvious.

_____ 5. The future belongs to whoever claims it.

_____ 6. Give whoever is going to Washington, D.C., directions to the National Museum of African Art.

_____ 7. What killed the dinosaurs is still uncertain.

_____ 8. Put whatever you need for the weekend in this suitcase.

_____ 9. Yes, you can write about whichever author you like.

_____ 10. Mr. Asato is who will be in charge of the field trip.

Copyright © by Holt, Rinehart and Winston. All rights reserved.

| LANGUAGE HANDBOOK | **7** | CLAUSES |

WORKSHEET 5 Test (Rules 7 a–f)

EXERCISE A Identify the italicized word group in each of the following sentences as either an independent clause or a subordinate clause. On the line provided, write *IND* for independent clause or *SUB* for subordinate clause.

EXAMPLE ___SUB___ **1.** The foundation must be strengthened *so that it can bear more weight.*

_____ **1.** Before I met Mumtaz, I didn't know anything about India, but *now I have learned much about that country.*

_____ **2.** Tell me *what you know about Venn diagrams.*

_____ **3.** The ship, *whose cargo was now on the ocean floor,* had to continue on its charted course.

_____ **4.** Early settlers owed much to American Indians, *who cultivated many plants unknown to Europeans.*

_____ **5.** *These flowers open* as soon as the sun goes down.

_____ **6.** *Do you know* where the wild strawberries grow?

_____ **7.** *It's easy* when you know how.

_____ **8.** *Where we would go this weekend* was the topic of the hour.

_____ **9.** Peace, *which has long been sought by both sides,* now appears close.

_____ **10.** *Until you have been in space,* you cannot imagine the beauty of our planet seen from a distance.

EXERCISE B Most of the following word groups are subordinate clauses. On the line provided, add an independent clause to each subordinate clause to make a clear and complete sentence. If the word group is an independent clause, rewrite it, punctuating and capitalizing it appropriately.

EXAMPLE **1.** where I grew up
        The town where I grew up has grown a great deal.

1. whose crops include coffee, oranges, and sugar cane

_____

2. dragonflies flitted over the tops of the roses

_____

3. which he called yesterday

_____

Continued ☞

Copyright © by Holt, Rinehart and Winston. All rights reserved.

4. since her parents gave her a curfew

_____

5. whoever requests assistance

_____

6. that Earl found on the sidewalk

_____

7. before the telegraph was invented

_____

8. when my bicycle chain broke

_____

9. whatever you like

_____

10. was this choice wisely made

_____

EXERCISE C   Most of the following sentences contain subordinate clauses. Underline each subordinate clause. If a sentence does not have a subordinate clause, write *IND* for independent on the line provided.

EXAMPLE _____ **1.** We are so proud of you and all <u>that you have accomplished</u>.

_____ **1.** If the Panama Canal had not been constructed, shipping between the Atlantic and Pacific Oceans would have been greatly delayed.

_____ **2.** Since airplanes were invented, many ancient sites have been discovered by alert pilots.

_____ **3.** Peru, whose Andes Mountains rise into the clouds, long ago used efficient methods of farming.

_____ **4.** What you see is a magnificent view of the Grand Canyon.

_____ **5.** The most efficient machine is whichever one uses the least energy to perform the most work.

_____ **6.** Sailors could more safely venture beyond sight of land after the compass came into use.

_____ **7.** On Monday, we will discuss the importance of the Baltic Sea, which separates Scandinavia from the rest of northern Europe.

Copyright © by Holt, Rinehart and Winston. All rights reserved.

Continued ☞

_____ 8. Screwdrivers, which are based on the principle of the lever, come in various shapes and sizes.

_____ 9. Can you name two animals that are found in Tasmania?

_____ 10. Where is the Ross Sea, and for whom is it named?

EXERCISE D   Underline the subordinate clause in each of the following sentences. On the line provided, write how the clause is being used. Write *N* for noun, *ADJ* for adjective, or *ADV* for adverb.

EXAMPLE ___N___ 1. <u>Wherever I am</u> is home to me.

_____ 1. Thunder boomed four seconds after a huge lightning bolt split the sky.

_____ 2. Because Argentina possesses such rich grasslands, cattle ranches prosper.

_____ 3. Turn right at the first stop sign that you see.

_____ 4. Whenever the magnet passed over the compass, the compass needle spun wildly.

_____ 5. You must do whatever you want most.

_____ 6. Did you know that the Colossus of Rhodes was one of the Seven Wonders of the Ancient World?

_____ 7. Who were the people whose manuscripts have been discovered in the deserts of the Middle East?

_____ 8. African drums may sound mysterious to people who are not used to hearing them.

_____ 9. Do you know what alphabet has the most letters?

_____ 10. The world is full of things that are invisible and unknown to us.

EXERCISE E   Underline the noun clause in each of the following sentences. Then, on the line provided, write how the clause is used in the sentence. Use the following abbreviations: Write *S* for subject, *IO* for indirect object, *DO* for direct object, *PN* for predicate nominative, or *OP* for object of a preposition.

EXAMPLE ___DO___ 1. Do you know <u>where a printer can be repaired</u>?

_____ 1. Do you think that we can visit El Pueblo de Los Angeles State Historical Park during our trip to California?

_____ 2. You can give whomever you like these extra tickets.

_____ 3. Because of gravity, what goes up comes down.

_____ 4. Scouts, make a shelter from whatever you can find.

_____ 5. That's what I like about chemistry.

Copyright © by Holt, Rinehart and Winston. All rights reserved.

LANGUAGE HANDBOOK 8 SENTENCES

WORKSHEET 1 | **Sentence or Sentence Fragment? (Rule 8 a)**

EXERCISE A Some of the following word groups are sentences, although none of the word groups have beginning capital letters or end punctuation. On the line provided, write *S* if the word group is a sentence or *F* if it is a fragment.

EXAMPLE ___F___ **1.** running to catch the bus

_____ **1.** she drove to Mexico City to see the Ballet Folklorico

_____ **2.** three business leaders organized a fund-raising drive

_____ **3.** saying that *kimchi* was her favorite Korean dish

_____ **4.** the mountain road had a hairpin turn

_____ **5.** before doing any of the extra-credit problems

_____ **6.** the cost of a new car and the cost of a used car

_____ **7.** stayed up watching the city fireworks display

_____ **8.** a red light blinking on and off at the top of the tower

_____ **9.** we got lost during the nature hike

_____ **10.** her shouts echoed against the steep canyon walls

EXERCISE B In each of the following word groups, underline the word or words in parentheses that make the word group a complete sentence.

EXAMPLE **1.** The team (*competing*, *competed*) in a track event.

1. Kenesha and Chim (*run*, *running*) long distances.

2. (*And*, *They*) practice on an outdoor track at school.

3. Why must they (*stretch*, *stretching*) their muscles before running?

4. (*Because warm-ups*, *Warm-ups*) make them limber.

5. (*They both*, *Since they*) will run in the race next week.

6. The race (*taking*, *will take*) place at Longwood Track Club.

7. A gold medal (*is*, *being*) the first prize.

8. (*And*, *Someone*) might break the track record.

9. Kenesha (*has*, *having*) never raced before.

10. (*She says*, *Saying*) that she is very excited about the race.

Copyright © by Holt, Rinehart and Winston. All rights reserved.

Elements of Literature

LANGUAGE HANDBOOK 8 SENTENCES

| WORKSHEET 2 | Identifying Sentence Fragments (Rule 8 a)

EXERCISE A   The following word groups are written as sentences, but some are actually sentence fragments. On the line provided, write *S* if the word group is a sentence or *F* if the word group is a sentence fragment.

EXAMPLE __F__ **1.** Gilgamesh, the hero of the epic poem.

_____ **1.** At the foot of the tallest mountain.

_____ **2.** The lights were visible at the foot of the tallest mountain.

_____ **3.** Three blackbirds sitting on a fence.

_____ **4.** Thi and I saw three blackbirds sitting on a fence.

_____ **5.** A quarterback famous for his ability on offense.

_____ **6.** The flag flapping gently in the morning breeze.

_____ **7.** The Chinese poet Li Po wrote "Quiet Night Thoughts."

_____ **8.** Breakfast cereal without fruit.

_____ **9.** Kino, Juana, and Coyotito, the principal characters of John Steinbeck's novel *The Pearl*.

_____ **10.** It was Margaret O'Reilly herself.

EXERCISE B   On the line provided, rewrite each of the following sentence fragments, adding whatever words and punctuation are necessary to make a complete sentence.

EXAMPLE **1.** Dr. Hugh Morgan Hill, an African American storyteller.

Dr. Hugh Morgan Hill, an African American storyteller, is
better known as Brother Blue.

1. before the end of the program

_____

2. the chair next to the fireplace

_____

3. but never came back again

_____

4. asked Reverend Jesse Jackson about his ambitions

_____

5. a kachina doll that my grandfather had made

_____

Copyright © by Holt, Rinehart and Winston. All rights reserved.

LANGUAGE HANDBOOK 8 SENTENCES

WORKSHEET 3 | **Identifying Complete Sentences (Rule 8 a)**

EXERCISE A   On the line to the left of each word group below, write *S* if the word group is a sentence or *F* if it is a sentence fragment.

EXAMPLE __*F*__ 1. Plato, who was the founder of the Academy in Athens.

_____ **1.** While Tom Sawyer was wandering around in the cave.

_____ **2.** Because she thought she was not tall enough, Kelley did not try out for the basketball team.

_____ **3.** Candace found the trail when she reached the mouth of the canyon.

_____ **4.** As we read "The Guitar" by Federico García Lorca.

_____ **5.** Because Earline had been frightened by a bear near camp.

_____ **6.** While she was at camp last summer, Mari practiced lifesaving skills.

_____ **7.** Although an old boot and a can of beans were found in the cave.

_____ **8.** No one had lived there for many years.

_____ **9.** According to the sayings attributed to Confucius.

_____ **10.** The poetic image in the haiku.

EXERCISE B   The following paragraph contains sentence fragments. Correct each fragment by attaching it to the sentence with which it belongs. As necessary, cross out end marks and capital letters, and add commas and lowercase letters. *Note:* The revised paragraph should contain five sentences.

EXAMPLE Benjamin Franklin moved from Boston, Massachusetts, to
Philadelphia, Pennsylvania, When he was seventeen years old.

Benjamin Franklin began his famous publishing career in Philadelphia. The largest city

in colonial America. Through hard work and diligence. He bought the *Pennsylvania*

Gazette. A dull, poorly printed newspaper. By writing many of the articles himself.

Franklin made the newspaper amusing, lively, and informative. Later, in 1732, under the

pen name Richard Saunders. Franklin wrote the first issue of *Poor Richard's Almanack*.

Because of its wise and witty sayings. Franklin's almanac soon became the most popular

almanac in the colonies.

Copyright © by Holt, Rinehart and Winston. All rights reserved.

LANGUAGE HANDBOOK **8** **SENTENCES**

| WORKSHEET 4 | Correcting Sentence Fragments (Rule 8 a) |

EXERCISE   Each of the following items contains two word groups. If both word groups are sentences, write *S* on the line provided. If one of the word groups is a sentence fragment, write *F*. Then, correct the sentence fragment by attaching it to the other word group. Be sure to use correct capitalization and punctuation.

EXAMPLE   __F__   1. On my birthday we went to Great America. A large amusement park.

On my birthday we went to Great America, a large
amusement park.

_____ 1. Every year, the United States imports millions of pounds of bananas from Latin America. A leading banana-producing area. _____

_____ 2. They were not heard from for five years. They were lost in the jungle.

_____ 3. In the middle of the night, Alfredo was suddenly awakened. By a curious humming noise outside his window. _____

_____ 4. Carla is taking tai chi lessons. She attends the class twice a week. _____

_____ 5. For her novel about life in New England, Joan Blos won the Newbery Medal. An award for children's literature. _____

_____ 6. The salesperson told me. To wait at the front desk. _____

_____ 7. The next speaker was Dr. Widdicomb. A family doctor. _____

_____ 8. The bill will probably be defeated. Despite all the senator's efforts. _____

_____ 9. My sister is learning lacrosse. An American Indian game. _____

_____ 10. My parents asked me. To be home by 8:00 P.M. _____

Copyright © by Holt, Rinehart and Winston. All rights reserved.

LANGUAGE HANDBOOK **8** **SENTENCES**

WORKSHEET 5 **Finding Subjects and Predicates (Rules 8 b–d)**

EXERCISE A   Use a vertical line to separate the complete subject and the complete predicate in each of the following sentences.

EXAMPLE 1. Dad | bought a new car last week.

1. This new car is a blue-and-white four-door sedan.

2. It has a sunroof and an automatic transmission.

3. The leather seats feel comfortable.

4. Dual air bags make the car very safe.

5. Our family's new car is a small one with a big trunk.

6. It gets thirty miles per gallon of gas.

7. Consumers don't like to spend too much on gasoline.

8. Small cars use less gasoline than large vehicles.

9. Some owners of large cars have traded them for smaller models.

10. Many larger vehicles have an extra tax on them.

EXERCISE B   In each of the following sentences, underline the complete subject once and the complete predicate twice.

EXAMPLE 1. The lost child ran across the street to the police station.

1. In history class we discussed Sacagawea's role in the Lewis and Clark expedition.

2. Some people can speak both French and English.

3. The cut on Harry's foot kept him out of the game.

4. At a nearby table sat the actor Cuba Gooding, Jr.

5. Hardly any news reporters were present.

6. The lights in the houses along the shore came on one by one.

7. The lighthouse could be seen from the boat.

8. Two detectives questioned the suspect.

9. Down toward the pond a goose with six goslings waddled.

10. Did Ron Arias write *The Road to Tamazunchale*?

Copyright © by Holt, Rinehart and Winston. All rights reserved.

Copyright © by Holt, Rinehart and Winston. All rights reserved.

LANGUAGE HANDBOOK **8** SENTENCES

WORKSHEET 6 **Finding Complete Subjects, Simple Subjects, and Verbs (Rules 8 b–d)**

EXERCISE A   In each of the following sentences, underline the complete subject once and the verb, including any helping verbs, twice.

> **EXAMPLE 1.** Once again <u>our girls' basketball team</u> <u>has won</u> the state championship.

1. Four of my friends had won tickets to the Whitney Houston concert.

2. This car is powered by solar batteries.

3. At the back of your literature book is a glossary of literary terms.

4. The world's second-largest continent is Africa.

5. George will have already left for the movies.

6. Do you ever watch the game show *Where in Time Is Carmen Sandiego?*

7. At the bookstore the mystery writer will autograph copies of her new novel.

8. One of our favorite sports is basketball.

9. Tonight we can sleep in our tents.

10. Jorge sent the package to me by parcel post.

EXERCISE B   In each of the following sentences, underline the complete subject once and the verb, including any helping verbs, twice. Then, circle the simple subject.

> **EXAMPLE 1.** The (wolf) <u>is considered</u> a member of the dog family.

1. Throughout history, many people have feared the wolf.

2. Fables such as "Little Red Riding Hood" have given wolves a bad reputation.

3. The loud, mournful howling of wolves can be frightening, too.

4. Packs of wolves greet each other with howls before a hunt.

5. The howls of the wolves can also warn other wolves to stay away.

6. The quick, tireless, and clever wolves are excellent hunters.

7. The wolves strengthen elk and deer herds by eliminating weak animals.

8. Ranchers in areas with wolves dislike the animals for attacking their livestock.

9. Large numbers of wolves have been killed in the United States.

10. The endangered species is being reintroduced in some areas of the country.

Continued ☞

LANGUAGE HANDBOOK 8 WORKSHEET 6 (continued)

EXERCISE C   In each of the following sentences, underline the complete subject and then write the simple subject on the line provided.

> EXAMPLE   _strangers_   **1.** <u>Seven bearded strangers</u> walked into the sleepy New Mexico town.

_____ **1.** Apparently, the strangers were gold prospectors.

_____ **2.** Their sudden appearance quickly aroused the townspeople's curiosity.

_____ **3.** This quiet desert town had never seen such a sight.

_____ **4.** With keen interest the townspeople observed the prospectors' movements.

_____ **5.** Nobody in the town knew anything about the strangers.

_____ **6.** Down the street trudged the exhausted strangers.

_____ **7.** They went straight to the county clerk's office.

_____ **8.** Nothing could stop the hungry, thirsty men.

_____ **9.** Each of the prospectors filed a claim.

_____ **10.** These new claims lay together in the Sangre de Cristo Mountains.

_____ **11.** Several curious townspeople questioned the prospectors.

_____ **12.** The prospectors' answers did not satisfy the townspeople's curiosity.

_____ **13.** The exact location of their claims remained a secret.

_____ **14.** The silent, secretive group stayed in town.

_____ **15.** An ambitious young reporter from Taos met with the prospectors.

_____ **16.** The reporter's newspaper wanted their story.

_____ **17.** The editor of the paper promised the reporter a large bonus.

_____ **18.** The prospectors would not discuss their claims.

_____ **19.** The reporter's interview with the prospectors was unproductive.

_____ **20.** The secret of the seven prospectors was kept.

Copyright © by Holt, Rinehart and Winston. All rights reserved.

LANGUAGE
HANDBOOK **8** SENTENCES

WORKSHEET 7 Finding Verbs (Rules 8 a, b, d)

EXERCISE A   In each of the following sentences, draw a vertical line between the complete subject and the complete predicate. Then, underline the verb, including any helping verbs.

EXAMPLE **1.** A local artist | <u>visited</u> our school one day.

1. Pilar Hernández, a local artist, painted a picture of our school.

2. She titled the painting *Nuestra Escuela*.

3. She brought the painting to our school.

4. The artist asked a student for directions to the principal's office.

5. The principal's office had been moved.

6. The busy student had forgotten about the move.

7. He quickly gave the artist the wrong directions.

8. The principal noticed the confused stranger in the hallway.

9. The artist introduced herself.

10. The principal graciously accepted the beautiful painting.

EXERCISE B   Underline each of the verbs in the following paragraph. Be sure to include all the helping verbs.

EXAMPLE [1] Yesterday, the members of our fire department <u>faced</u> another emergency.

[1] Just before noon, the siren in the fire station sounded. [2] The fire department had received news of a major forest fire. [3] The fire had been raging for two hours already. [4] It was out of control. [5] The people at the scene called for help from the fire department. [6] It responded quickly. [7] The firefighters drove their trucks fifteen miles. [8] At the scene of the fire, they rushed their equipment into action. [9] They put their hoses into the river. [10] With the pumps on the trucks, they sprayed water onto the fire. [11] Because of the smoke, the firefighters could not breathe easily. [12] The smoke also made their eyes red. [13] Still, they fought the fire bravely. [14] Despite all their efforts, the heat from the fire forced the firefighters back. [15] Slowly, however, a change came over the sky. [16] Then, suddenly, rain poured down. [17] Torrents of rain quickly soaked the forest. [18] The firefighters rejoiced! [19] Without the rain the forest fire could have been a great disaster. [20] Instead, the fire was brought under control.

Copyright © by Holt, Rinehart and Winston. All rights reserved.

LANGUAGE HANDBOOK 8 SENTENCES

WORSHEET 8 | **Sentences with Compound Subjects and Compound Verbs (Rules 8 c–f)**

EXERCISE A   In the following sentences, underline each simple subject once and each verb twice.

> EXAMPLE   1. <u>Christopher Columbus</u> <u>was born</u> in Italy and <u>became</u> a sailor at fourteen.

1. Dad and I bought eggplant, zucchini, onions, green peppers, tomatoes, and garlic and made *ratatouille* for my French Club banquet.

2. Marie studied geography in school and read books about computers at home.

3. Some people have warned me about the dangers of in-line skating.

4. Bill Cosby's television programs and his books are both funny and inspirational.

5. The winner and the loser were both brave and intelligent.

6. The knight asked for the king's help but did not receive it.

7. My sister traveled to Peru and visited Cuzco, Arequipa, and Lima.

8. Before the American Revolution the British had fought a costly war against the French and won.

9. After the concert my friend and I hurried toward the bus.

10. Mercury served as messenger of the gods in Roman mythology and was the god of roads and travel.

EXERCISE B   In the following sentences, underline each subject. Then, write *CS* on the line to the left of each sentence that contains a compound subject.

> EXAMPLE   _*CS*_   1. A <u>dog</u> and then a <u>girl</u> with a leash raced past us.

_____   **1.** Many art lovers and collectors visit Sedona, Arizona, each year.

_____   **2.** Mother and I prepared *arroz con pollo* for dinner last night.

_____   **3.** The lights of the neon sign flashed brightly.

_____   **4.** The headlights of the oncoming cars were blinding.

_____   **5.** Tables and chairs were turned upside down.

_____   **6.** Jagged rocks and pieces of dirt fell on the roof.

_____   **7.** A clown and a juggler rode at the head of the Cinco de Mayo parade.

_____   **8.** Gordon and Pasqual dress as bears and serve as our team's mascots.

_____   **9.** Two hawks soared above the valley.

_____   **10.** A firefighter leaned out the window and dropped a small dog safely into the net below.

Copyright © by Holt, Rinehart and Winston. All rights reserved.

Elements of Literature

| WORKSHEET 9 | Test (Rules 8 a–f) |

EXERCISE A   Some of the following items are sentences, and others are sentence fragments. On the line provided, write *S* before each item that is a sentence and *F* before each item that is a sentence fragment.

EXAMPLE ___*F*___ **1.** Ricardo's collection of antique toys.

_____ **1.** Collecting antique toys can be both fun and profitable.

_____ **2.** For the sake of starting a collection.

_____ **3.** Merely because a toy appeals to you.

_____ **4.** Often antiques increase in value with age.

_____ **5.** A special toy of unusual design.

_____ **6.** Fun exploring the history of unique toys.

_____ **7.** This toy train from the 1890s is still in good condition.

_____ **8.** Examining the toy train and imagining previous owners.

_____ **9.** Other homemade toys are from the turn of the century.

_____ **10.** Because Ricardo and I have found that going to antique-toy shows makes history more vivid.

EXERCISE B   In the following sentences, underline each subject once and each verb twice, including any helping verbs.

EXAMPLE **1.** After the fall of Rome, <u>life</u> and <u>property</u> <u>were</u> unsafe.

1. In A.D. 350 the Huns crossed the Volga River and entered Europe.

2. They were a nomadic and warlike tribe from Asia.

3. In A.D. 451 Attila and the Huns swept across Europe.

4. Attila spared the city of Rome and then withdrew from Italy.

5. In A.D. 476 the Germans fought and defeated the Roman army.

6. The defeat of the Roman army was a disaster for the Roman Empire.

7. After the defeat of its army, the Roman Empire fell apart.

8. Historians study the collapse of the Roman Empire and write articles about the people and customs of that period of decline.

9. Poor Roman farmers would sell their lands and work for wealthy landowners.

10. In time these farmers became serfs and lost their private property.

Copyright © by Holt, Rinehart and Winston. All rights reserved.

LANGUAGE HANDBOOK **9** **COMPLEMENTS**

| WORKSHEET 1 | Finding Subjects, Verbs, and Complements (Rule 9 a)

EXERCISE In the following sentences, underline each subject once and each verb twice. Then, circle each complement. *Note:* Not every sentence contains a complement.

EXAMPLE **1.** The <u>newspaper</u> in our town <u>held</u> a disc golf (contest.)

1. The judges announced a set of rules.

2. The rules were simple.

3. The judges created three contest divisions.

4. The first division involved games between two players.

5. The second division tested distance.

6. The winner threw the disc with great power.

7. The last division involved a test of accuracy.

8. Discs were hurled into a basket.

9. Both Salvatore and Annetta entered the contest.

10. Annetta practiced steadily for a week.

11. This was her first contest.

12. Sometimes she and Salvatore practiced together.

13. Salvatore had competed for the past two years.

14. The day of the contest arrived.

15. Both Salvatore and Annetta were nervous.

16. Salvatore entered the third division.

17. He did not win.

18. Annetta joined the first-division competition.

19. She was defeated by a more experienced contestant.

20. Annetta and Salvatore will compete again next year.

Copyright © by Holt, Rinehart and Winston. All rights reserved.

WORKSHEET 2 | Finding Direct Objects (Rules 9 a, b)

EXERCISE A   In each of the following sentences, underline the subject once and the verb twice. Then, draw an arrow from the verb to the direct object.

EXAMPLE   **1.** Mr. Wilcox had read some of the books.

1. They planted six beds of tulips in the garden.

2. A bolt of lightning split the tree down the middle.

3. The heavy rain washed the soil away from the dinosaur bones.

4. Can Geraldo recite the first paragraph of the Gettysburg Address?

5. Tranh ordered chicken gumbo at the Cajun restaurant.

6. The city put a fence of redwood planks along the road.

7. Has Kelli tasted the spicy crawfish gumbo?

8. Our team successfully blocked the kick.

9. Aola plays the violin in the school orchestra.

10. The undercover agent delivered the package of microfilm to the contact.

EXERCISE B   Underline every direct object in the following paragraph. *Note:* Not all of the sentences have direct objects; some have more than one direct object.

EXAMPLE   [1] Have you heard this story?

[1] The ancient Greeks told a story about a musical contest between the god Pan and the god Apollo. [2] Pan played pipes of reed, and Apollo played a silver lyre. [3] Pan and Apollo sang songs, and then they demanded a decision from their audience. [4] The mountain god Tmolus gave the award to Apollo, but Midas, the king of Lydia, preferred Pan. [5] Apollo was very angry. [6] He changed Midas's ears into donkey's ears. [7] One should favor the stronger god in contests between two gods! [8] Midas hid his ugly ears under his cap. [9] His barber discovered the dreadful secret. [10] Midas threatened the barber with punishment if he told. [11] The barber could not resist the urge to tell. [12] He dug a hole at the river and then whispered the secret into the hole. [13] He covered the hole containing the secret with earth. [14] However, reeds grew up there. [15] Every time the wind blew, the reeds whispered the secret of Midas. [16] "Midas has donkey's ears." [17] The whole country eventually heard the secret, and Midas was covered with shame. [18] We don't know Midas's fate. [19] The story does not describe it. [20] Perhaps Apollo relented.

Copyright © by Holt, Rinehart and Winston. All rights reserved.

LANGUAGE
HANDBOOK **9** **COMPLEMENTS**

| WORSHEET 3 | **Identifying Direct Objects and Indirect Objects (Rules 9 a–c)** |

EXERCISE   Underline each indirect object once and each direct object twice in each of the following sentences. Remember that a sentence can contain more than one indirect or direct object.

          EXAMPLE **1.** Send <u>Otis</u> and <u>us</u> a <u>postcard</u> from the Rocky Mountains!

1. Could you design us a chart in three dimensions?

2. Wow! That Web site surely gave me a lot of information.

3. Take your sister today's newspaper.

4. Who taught you weaving?

5. Our sources give the bill every chance of passing in the Senate.

6. They taught their students the importance and usefulness of writing skills.

7. Aunt Ruth promised Carl and her another chance to see the Renoir exhibit.

8. We could make Mom and Dad supper tonight and surprise them.

9. That evening, Mr. Marcado sold the company a three-story building.

10. In honor of her election, they gave her a gavel.

11. Pass him the ball!

12. Who ordered us tacos?

13. Could they grant him a special visa to China?

14. Read me a story about the fire keeper.

15. Mrs. Rogers assigned Cynthia and the rest of the class two papers and an experiment.

16. Please tell me the time.

17. Would you lend me money for a phone call, Dena?

18. Test officials will issue you all necessary supplies for the examination.

19. She drew us a picture of her dream.

20. Would you show Ambassador Chen and her husband their room?

Copyright © by Holt, Rinehart and Winston. All rights reserved.

LANGUAGE
HANDBOOK **9** COMPLEMENTS

WORSHEET 4 | **Linking Verbs and Subject Complements**
(Rules 9 d, e)

EXERCISE A   Complete each of the following sentences by writing an appropriate linking verb in the blank. Try not to use the same verb twice. Some linking verbs may require a helping verb.

EXAMPLE 1. Ahanu ___must be___ very happy.

1. Ming Chin _____ sleepy listening to the music.

2. The moon _____ bigger through a telescope.

3. On rainy days I usually _____ lazy.

4. The cat _____ friendlier as we brushed its fur.

5. The old Spanish castle _____ weather-beaten.

6. The grilled onions _____ delicious.

7. Leslie _____ undecided, even after her friends' encouragement.

8. The pounding hail _____ very loud on the roof.

9. Will the chili _____ too hot if I add more peppers?

10. Despite all the noise, the toddler _____ asleep.

EXERCISE B   In the following sentences, underline each linking verb once; underline each subject complement twice. Then, on the line provided, write *PN* if the complement is a predicate nominative or *PA* if it is a predicate adjective. A sentence may have more than one complement.

EXAMPLE ___PA___ **1.** <u>Does</u> the molded gelatin salad <u>look firm</u> to you?

_____ **1.** One of the U.S. senators from this state is a woman.

_____ **2.** The hot cereal and fresh toast smelled delicious.

_____ **3.** Imogene appears unusually cheerful this morning.

_____ **4.** His favorite sports are soccer and field hockey.

_____ **5.** Because of her exercising, Anita is becoming stronger.

_____ **6.** The breed of the prize-winning milk cow was Guernsey.

_____ **7.** Sandy's new interest is food from other cultures.

_____ **8.** My pet gerbil, Hercules, is tan.

_____ **9.** The milk quickly turned sour in the warm kitchen.

_____ **10.** The students seem curious about the Lewis and Clark expedition.

Copyright © by Holt, Rinehart and Winston. All rights reserved.

WORKSHEET 5 | Identifying Predicate Nominatives and Predicate Adjectives (Rules 9 d, e)

EXERCISE Underline the linking verb in each of the following sentences. Then, on the line provided, write each subject complement. Label each complement either *PA* for predicate adjective or *PN* for predicate nominative. *Note:* Not every sentence will have both a predicate adjective and a predicate nominative; some sentences may have more than one of either.

> **EXAMPLE** **1.** Yes, she <u>is</u> a doctor—and very interesting, too.
>
> *doctor, PN; interesting, PA*

1. The Leaning Tower of Pisa is a demonstration of the rule that buildings need to stand up straight.

_____

2. Even well into her seventies, she remained a tireless worker and a brilliant thinker.

_____

3. This machine is efficient; it is also one of a kind.

_____

4. In Sri Lanka, coconut palms grow tall and produce beautiful fruit.

_____

5. Freshly cut grass smells sweet.

_____

6. The sea is essential to Japan's economy and food supply.

_____

7. My favorite movie has always been *Star Wars*.

_____

8. Wole Soyinka is an African playwright and one voice for the Nigerian people.

_____

9. They were happy in their hometown in Taiwan.

_____

10. The rice fields looked well tended and productive.

_____

Copyright © by Holt, Rinehart and Winston. All rights reserved.

WORKSHEET 6 | Test (Rules 9 a–e)

EXERCISE A In the following sentences, underline each subject once and each verb twice. Circle each complement. Sentences may have compound subjects, compound verbs, and more than one complement.

EXAMPLE 1. A Zuni legend tells an interesting (story) about the origin of winter.

1. Coyote and Eagle were travelers together.

2. One day, the people in a Zuni pueblo bid them welcome.

3. Coyote noticed two boxes in the pueblo.

4. The Zunis kept the sun in one box and the moon in the other.

5. Eagle put the sun and the moon together in one box and flew off with them.

6. Coyote repeatedly pestered Eagle about the box.

7. Finally, Eagle gave Coyote the box.

8. Coyote accidentally released the sun and the moon from the box.

9. The sun and moon took their heat far away from the earth.

10. In this way, Coyote brought winter into the world.

EXERCISE B In the following sentences, underline each subject once and each verb twice. Circle each complement. Sentences may have compound subjects, compound verbs, and more than one complement.

EXERCISE 1. Are dolphins and whales (mammals) or (fish)?

1. Dolphins, porpoises, and whales are members of the same group of mammals.

2. Dolphins inhabit fresh water or salt water, depending on their species.

3. A highly developed sense of hearing and the ability to click and whistle are the dolphins' communications tools.

4. When hunting, the intelligent dolphins make clicking sounds and analyze the echoes that return.

5. Scientists and the general public remain fascinated and feel challenged to learn about these complex animals.

Copyright © by Holt, Rinehart and Winston. All rights reserved.

Continued ☞

EXERCISE C   In the following sentences, underline each direct object once, underline each indirect object twice, and circle each subject complement. *Note:* Sentences may have more than one complement.

> **EXAMPLES** 1. The sword in the stone was a great (mystery.)
>
>   2. The sword played a large part in the history of England.
>
>   3. The sword has also given us a wonderful legend.

1. Many years ago, a churchyard in England contained a strange monument.

2. The monument was a sword stuck into a great stone.

3. According to legend, the next king of England would pull the sword from the stone.

4. On New Year's Day, all the knights held a tournament.

5. One of the knights in the tournament was Sir Kay.

6. While getting ready for the contest, he could not find his sword.

7. His weapon was missing.

8. He called his younger brother.

9. "Arthur, would you get me my sword?"

10. Arthur, however, could not find Sir Kay's sword at home.

11. On the way back to the tournament, Arthur remembered the sword in the churchyard.

12. With no one around, Arthur pulled the sword out of the stone.

13. He would return the sword after the tournament.

14. At the tournament, Sir Kay recognized the weapon as the sword from the stone.

15. All the knights followed Sir Kay and Arthur back to the churchyard.

16. Arthur put the sword back into the stone.

17. Neither Sir Kay nor any of the other knights could pull out the sword.

18. Arthur easily removed the sword from the stone.

19. All the knights offered Arthur their loyalty.

20. Arthur became the king of England.

Copyright © by Holt, Rinehart and Winston. All rights reserved.

| WORKSHEET 1 | **Finding Subjects and Verbs in Simple Sentences (Rule 10 a)** |

EXERCISE A   In each of the following simple sentences, underline the subject or subjects once and the verb or verbs twice.

> EXAMPLE **1.** <u>Dozens</u> of ears of corn <u>sat</u> in a pile near a large outdoor oven.

1. Mr. Trujillo cherished the old photograph of his grandfather.

2. A small mariachi band and a few listeners stood on the sidewalk.

3. Sage and a few cacti dotted the rocky outcrop and offered shelter to lizards, snakes, and rabbits.

4. Later the corn would be ground into meal and made into tortillas.

5. A lace mantilla and a red rose completed the bride's costume.

6. A week's laundry was pinned to a clothesline.

7. Men, women, and children thronged the market, admired the goods, and enjoyed the atmosphere.

8. Trees without leaves clung to the banks of the narrow creek.

9. Silver bracelets, belts, and earrings lined the walls and counters of the shop in Mexico City.

10. With steady hands, she lifted the basketball and made the free throw.

11. Headlights and yellowish streetlights lit up the adobe buildings.

12. Will *Barrio Boy* be on the reading list this year?

13. On the way to the market, she and Elena hung their shopping bags over their arms.

14. The woman and her son rushed together, embraced, and smiled happily.

15. From the tin chimney wafted a thin stream of smoke.

16. The sky over the Pecos River blazed red and violet in the sunset.

17. The woman carrying an umbrella took the smoked fish and wrapped it in newspaper.

18. Red and green tassels hung from the brim of her hat and bobbed up and down with her every step.

19. Using only a rope halter, the boy shifted his weight and guided the horse with his legs.

20. Out of the pickup truck came the harsh sounds of an untuned guitar and an off-key song.

Copyright © by Holt, Rinehart and Winston. All rights reserved.

Continued ☞

LANGUAGE HANDBOOK **10** **WORKSHEET 1** *(continued)*

EXERCISE B On the line provided, write the subject(s) and verb(s) of each of the following simple sentences. Label each subject *S* and each verb *V*.

> **EXAMPLE 1.** Did the rancher carry the calf into the barn?
>
> *rancher, S; Did carry, V*

1. Two fallen trees blocked the trail.

_____

2. The man and the girl each carried a dozen large plastic bottles down to the creek.

_____

3. A shower of raindrops fell on the horse and rider and, within a few minutes, soaked them thoroughly.

_____

4. Metal roofs are practical and durable and, best of all, make a lovely sound in a rainstorm.

_____

5. Long black braids and a center part framed Julia's face and gave her an air of neatness and honesty.

_____

EXERCISE C In each of the following simple sentences, underline the subject or subjects once and the verb or verbs twice.

> **EXAMPLE 1.** Have Roger and Ellen ever seen a barbed wire fence?

1. Shrubs with thorny barbs were used as fences for livestock by early settlers.
2. The Osage orange shrub inspired the development of barbed wire.
3. In 1874, Joseph Glidden of De Kalb, Illinois, brought barbed wire to the commercial market.
4. Homesteaders could fence their land and corral their animals with the new barbed wire.
5. The barbed wire fences protected the homesteaders' land from large herds of cattle and spelled the end of the open range.

Copyright © by Holt, Rinehart and Winston. All rights reserved.

Elements of Literature

WORKSHEET 2 | Identifying Subjects and Verbs in Compound Sentences (Rule 10 b)

EXERCISE A   In each of the following compound sentences, underline each subject once and each verb twice.

EXAMPLES 1. Shadows of palm trees decorate the walls; weary travelers sometimes rest in the trees' shade.

2. The intense sun shines on the parks and gardens, and the pink clay buildings contrast with the blue sky.

1. Marrakech may be very different from your hometown, but the city of many mosques is also very beautiful.

2. You have probably heard of Casablanca; it is situated on the northwest coast of Morocco.

3. Morocco borders the Mediterranean Sea and the Atlantic Ocean, yet fresh water is scarce.

4. Fishermen ply their trade in the ocean; several types of fish, such as tuna and sardines, are plentiful there.

5. Do Barbary pirates still patrol the coast of North Africa, or do they rest in a watery grave?

6. The Strait of Gibraltar separates Morocco from Spain; in ancient times, the strait was known as the Pillars of Hercules.

7. Ramadan is a time of fasting, so for one month Moroccan Muslims, like Muslims everywhere, do not eat or drink from dawn to dusk.

8. Over half of the Moroccan population is under twenty; many Moroccans have moved to western Europe in search of jobs.

9. Many old Moroccan buildings are mosques with square minarets, but other buildings are forts with low arches.

10. Morocco gained its independence from France in 1956, and the country is now a constitutional monarchy.

Continued ☞

Copyright © by Holt, Rinehart and Winston. All rights reserved.

EXERCISE B   On the line provided, write the subject(s) and verb(s) of each of the
following compound sentences. Label each subject *S* and each verb *V*.

> EXAMPLE **1.** Many people use computers today, and even more will
> learn about them soon.
>
> *people, S; use, V; more, S; will learn, V*

1. Computers are a part of everyday life; many schools now use computers.

_____

2. Today, many first-graders use computers, and some six-year-olds have even taught their
parents about computers.

_____

3. Schools are connecting to the World Wide Web; libraries in other countries can be
used by students from all over the world.

_____

4. Parents can check a school Web site from home; student assignments and
announcements are sometimes available at such Web sites.

_____

5. A student in Anchorage, Alaska, can send e-mail to a student in India, or the Alaskan
student can write a note to a friend next door.

_____

6. Computers are helping students, but their help may be costly.

_____

7. The World Wide Web is vast and complicated, yet it can be easy to use.

_____

8. The World Wide Web may be part of your work someday, for more and more
businesses are using Web sites.

_____

9. Computers connect the world's people; people in different countries can work together.

_____

10. Many users of the World Wide Web communicate in English; you will probably need
to know English very well.

_____

Copyright © by Holt, Rinehart and Winston. All rights reserved.

LANGUAGE
HANDBOOK **10** KINDS OF SENTENCES

WORKSHEET 3 | **Identifying Clauses in Complex Sentences**
(Rule 10 c)

EXERCISE   In each of the following complex sentences, underline each independent clause once and each subordinate clause twice.

EXAMPLE 1. Perched on his arm was the tiniest frog that I have ever seen.

1. I once saw a man who rode a horse up to a bank's drive-through window and cashed a check.

2. The file cabinet won't open unless you have the key.

3. When he had finished one book, Josh started another one.

4. I understand what you are saying.

5. When Rafael and Kumiko brushed against the shrub, a cloud of mosquitoes took flight.

6. On the kitchen cabinets were knobs that were shaped like tiny feet and hands.

7. A hundred walruses lay on the beach and sunned themselves before they entered the sea again.

8. Do you understand how the magician did that trick?

9. I talked with Nathan Jones, who dreams of designing a better backpack.

10. Twenty houses made up the tiny village that had only a dirt road.

11. As the breeze swept through the terrace, the music of the bamboo wind chimes drifted into the house.

12. If the litmus paper turns blue, is the solution acidic or alkaline?

13. The sea turtle returned to the ocean from which it came.

14. Many college graduates are drawn to the opportunities that software companies offer.

15. Because that woman was wearing surgical scrubs, I thought she was a doctor.

16. She made the basket just before the buzzer sounded.

17. My socks didn't match because I had dressed in the dark that morning.

18. The scholarships are provided by Mr. Takeshi, whose generosity is well-known.

19. At the bottom of the muddy river lived a huge catfish that had avoided capture for a long time.

20. Although you might enjoy pizza every day, you should eat a variety of foods.

Copyright © by Holt, Rinehart and Winston. All rights reserved.

LANGUAGE
HANDBOOK **10** KINDS OF SENTENCES

WORKSHEET 4	**Classifying Sentences by Structure and Purpose**

(Rules 10 a–g)

EXERCISE A   Classify each of the following sentences. On the line provided, write *DECL* if the sentence is declarative, *INTER* if it is interrogative, *IMPER* if it is imperative, or *EXCL* if it is exclamatory. Then, add the appropriate end punctuation.

EXAMPLE ___*IMPER*___ **1.** Make way for the captain*!* (*or* captain*.*)

_____ **1.** Do you want Parmesan cheese on your pasta

_____ **2.** Suddenly, a flashlight beam cut through the darkness

_____ **3.** I chased the squirrel out of the house

_____ **4.** What a lovely day this is

_____ **5.** Do not overcook ramen, or the noodles will turn to sticky mush

_____ **6.** Use a roller to paint large, flat surfaces

_____ **7.** A glass top protected the tablecloth and the wood underneath it

_____ **8.** We loved that book

_____ **9.** The author of *The House on Mango Steet* is Sandra Cisneros

_____ **10.** Make a schedule, and stick to it

EXERCISE B   Classify each of the following sentences. On the line provided, write *S* if it is a simple sentence, *CD* if it is a compound sentence, or *CX* if it is a complex sentence.

EXAMPLE ___*CX*___ **1.** Respect for each other's differences is what makes civilization possible.

_____ **1.** The leaves of the plant were so large that I didn't notice the geckos.

_____ **2.** Birds flew, children played, and the sun shone.

_____ **3.** My sister has a paper route, and I help her deliver papers every morning.

_____ **4.** Later that evening, Lucy and I stood at the wishing well and made a wish.

_____ **5.** Rollers crush raw latex into sheets of rubber, which are then dried.

_____ **6.** Mangroves provide nectar for honeybees.

_____ **7.** Bright, colored neon lights blinked on and off as we drove through town.

_____ **8.** A hollow gourd makes a great bird feeder; my feeder attracted lots of birds.

_____ **9.** A ceiling fan rotated slowly above us.

_____ **10.** On shelves sat a dozen of Vernon's model cars; each one was the result of many hours of work.

Copyright © by Holt, Rinehart and Winston. All rights reserved.

LANGUAGE HANDBOOK	**10**	KINDS OF SENTENCES

WORKSHEET 5 | Test (Rules 10 a–g)

EXERCISE A   In the following sentences, underline each subject once and each verb twice.

> **EXAMPLE 1.** <u>Acorns</u> and <u>twigs</u> <u>spilled</u> out of my little brother's lunch box.

1. After the clay is mixed, it must be kept moist.

2. The Ivory Coast was their destination; the stars were their only guide.

3. There may be answers to all life's mysteries, but we do not know them yet.

4. The Fourth of July is my favorite holiday.

5. Gardeners sometimes cut back a weak plant so that it will grow back more vigorously.

6. He did not become a naturalist; he was born one.

7. Was *Star Wars* or *The Empire Strikes Back* more exciting?

8. This Navajo basket, which was lent to us by a museum, will be displayed in the lobby.

9. Ulysses tried to find his way home for many years.

10. Do you understand that you must call first?

EXERCISE B   Identify the italicized clause in each of the following sentences. On the line provided, write *S* for subordinate clause or *I* for independent clause.

> **EXAMPLE __I__ 1.** Since the flower bed has been mulched, *we need not weed it.*

_____ **1.** Recycling is good for the environment *because it helps conserve our resources.*

_____ **2.** These seats belong to *whoever comes first.*

_____ **3.** The film, *which was set in Africa,* was actually filmed in Brazil.

_____ **4.** After Dad and Aunt Millie mixed the concrete in a wheelbarrow, *I poured it into the mold.*

_____ **5.** *If we paint the room green,* the red curtains won't match.

_____ **6.** *You may write a song* when you are trying to write a poem.

_____ **7.** The Polynesian chorus *to which I'm referring* is available on compact disc.

_____ **8.** Although children learn languages more quickly than adults, *people of any age can learn a new language.*

_____ **9.** *Eventually, the company hired a person* who had two years' experience with computers.

_____ **10.** Can you prove *that ice is a crystal?*

Continued ☞

Copyright © by Holt, Rinehart and Winston. All rights reserved.

EXERCISE C   Identify each of the following sentences. On the line provided, write *S* if it is a simple sentence, *CD* if it is a compound sentence, or *CX* if it is a complex sentence.

EXAMPLE ___*S*___ **1.** All at the same time, a hundred balloons flew up in the air.

_____ **1.** We took the clock to an antique dealer, and she valued it at over five hundred dollars.

_____ **2.** Henry Louis Gates, Jr., and Cornel West wrote a book together and teach at the W.E.B. Du Bois Institute at Harvard.

_____ **3.** Right after the bus pulled up, twelve women in basketball uniforms got out.

_____ **4.** Ramps and handrails help everyone, not just people who use wheelchairs or crutches.

_____ **5.** Static interrupted our call to Korea, so we hung up and dialed again.

_____ **6.** Overnight, a spider had spun a web that glistened with dew in the morning light.

_____ **7.** The capitol's dome rises high above the street; people can see it from far away.

_____ **8.** Her sister's mother-in-law is my teacher.

_____ **9.** Don't leave your glasses on the chair; somebody will sit on them.

_____ **10.** After the wild ponies were rounded up, we put them in the corral.

EXERCISE D   Identify each of the following sentences. On the line provided, write *DECL* if the sentence is declarative, *INTER* if it is interrogative, *IMPER* if it is imperative, or *EXCL* if it is exclamatory. Then, add appropriate end punctuation for each sentence.

EXAMPLE ___*DECL*___ **1.** Dad will show you how to knot that tie.

_____ **1.** How can you tell real kachina dolls from imitation ones

_____ **2.** Please excuse me

_____ **3.** The fanciful characters in *Alice's Adventures in Wonderland* came from the imagination of Lewis Carroll

_____ **4.** What a lucky break you got

_____ **5.** Call me tomorrow

_____ **6.** A row of basketball trophies shone on the mantel over the fireplace

_____ **7.** Go for it

_____ **8.** Wow, what a great skateboarder she is

_____ **9.** At what temperature does water boil

_____ **10.** How did that red sock get in the wash with my white T-shirts

Copyright © by Holt, Rinehart and Winston. All rights reserved.

LANGUAGE HANDBOOK **11** WRITING EFFECTIVE SENTENCES

WORKSHEET 1 | Combining Sentences (Rule 11 a)

EXERCISE A   Combine each of the following groups of sentences into one sentence, and write the complete sentence on the lines provided.

> **EXAMPLE 1.** Lobstering is a business.
>
> It is an exciting business. _Lobstering is an exciting business._

1. Captain Rollins goes out in the boat.

   The boat is large. _____

   _____

2. There is a winch on the boat.

   The winch is electric. _____

   _____

3. The winch pulls up the lobster trap.

   The lobster trap is heavy.

   The winch is powerful. _____

   _____

4. Captain Rollins takes the lobster from the trap.

   The lobster is live. _____

   _____

5. She uses meat or fish heads to catch the lobster.

   The meat is old.

   The fish heads are smelly. _____

   _____

6. She then drops the trap back to the bottom.

   The trap is baited.

   The bottom is rocky. _____

   _____

7. The lobster smells the bait in the trap.

   The lobster is hungry.

   The bait smells delicious. _____

   _____

Copyright © by Holt, Rinehart and Winston. All rights reserved.

Continued ☞

8. The lobster crawls into the trap and eats the bait.

 The lobster is hungry.

 The trap is open.

 The bait appears appetizing. _____

 _____

 _____

9. However, the lobster cannot crawl out of the passage in the trap.

 The lobster is well fed.

 The passage is one-way. _____

 _____

 _____

10. The lobster trap must be checked often.

 Lobsters have strong claws.

 Two lobsters in the same trap may injure or kill each other. _____

 _____

 _____

EXERCISE B   Combine each of the following groups of sentences into one sentence, and write the complete sentence on the lines provided.

 EXAMPLE **1.** Carlos speaks two languages.

  He speaks them well. *Carlos speaks two languages well.*

  _____

1. Carlos came from Puerto Rico.

 Carlos came here.

 He came recently. _____

 _____

 _____

2. Speaking two or more languages is a valuable skill.

 Speaking languages fluently is valuable.

 It is an extremely valuable skill. _____

 _____

 _____

Copyright © by Holt, Rinehart and Winston. All rights reserved.

LANGUAGE HANDBOOK **11** WRITING EFFECTIVE SENTENCES

WORKSHEET 2 | Combining Sentences (Rule 11 a)

EXERCISE   Combine each of the following groups of sentences into one sentence, and write the complete sentence on the lines provided.

> **EXAMPLE** **1.** Marguerite will be thirteen years old.
>
> Her birthday is in March.
>
> *Marguerite will be thirteen years old in March.* _____
>
> _____

1. Marguerite lives on a ranch.

The ranch is in Colorado. _____

_____

2. Marguerite's father inherited the ranch.

He inherited it from his grandfather. _____

_____

3. Marguerite's father raises sheep.

He raises them on the ranch. _____

_____

4. The sheep eat grass.

The grass is on the foothills.

The sheep eat the grass in summer. _____

_____

_____

5. The sheepherders are from the Basque region.

The Basque region is in Spain. _____

_____

_____

6. Marguerite likes to help the sheepherders.

She helps them with the lambs. _____

_____

_____

Continued ☞

Copyright © by Holt, Rinehart and Winston. All rights reserved.

7. Sometimes the weather is very cold.

It is cold in the mountains.

It is cold at lambing time. _____

_____

_____

8. Unless it stays with its mother, the lamb may become weak.

It may become weak during the first few days after birth.

It may become weak from lack of food. _____

_____

_____

9. Marguerite rides her horse.

She rides it around the ranch.

She rides it on errands. _____

_____

_____

10. Marguerite goes to school.

She goes after breakfast.

She goes by bus.

She goes to school in a nearby town. _____

_____

_____

_____

Copyright © by Holt, Rinehart and Winston. All rights reserved.

LANGUAGE HANDBOOK **11** WRITING EFFECTIVE SENTENCES

WORKSHEET 3 | Combining Sentences (Rule 11 a)

EXERCISE Combine each of the following groups of sentences by writing one complete sentence with a compound subject, a compound verb, or both a compound subject and a compound verb.

> EXAMPLE **1.** Juan Ponce de León sailed north from Puerto Rico.
>
> He explored the area that is now Florida.
>
> *Juan Ponce de León sailed north from Puerto Rico and*
>
> *explored the area that is now Florida.*

1. Joe "King" Oliver played jazz music.

Louis Armstrong played jazz music. _____

_____

_____

2. The Pilgrims landed at Plymouth in 1620.

They sought the friendship of the native Wampanoag people. _____

_____

_____

3. Hurricanes cause severe damage.

Tornadoes cause severe damage.

Blizzards cause severe damage. _____

_____

_____

4. Armand might bring the canoe down to the lake.

Paul might bring the canoe down to the lake. _____

_____

_____

5. Bianca wants to become a musician.

Linda wants to become a musician.

They have been studying music at school. _____

_____

_____

Copyright © by Holt, Rinehart and Winston. All rights reserved.

LANGUAGE HANDBOOK 11 WRITING EFFECTIVE SENTENCES

| WORKSHEET 4 | **Combining Sentences (Rule 11 a)** |

EXERCISE   Combine each of the following pairs of sentences by writing one compound sentence on the lines provided. Add commas where necessary.

EXAMPLE **1.** These flowering plants are beautiful.

Each requires special care.

These flowering plants are beautiful, but each requires special care.

1. Climates vary in the United States.

Different plants grow in each climate. _____

_____

_____

2. Some plants thrive in hot and humid weather.

Other varieties prefer a cooler, drier climate. _____

_____

_____

3. Gardeners plant tulip bulbs in the early fall.

In the early spring small sprouts appear. _____

_____

_____

4. Pine trees can grow in many climates.

Varieties of these evergreens fill the forests of North America. _____

_____

_____

5. The loblolly pine is a familiar sight in the South.

In the North other types of pine are more common. _____

_____

_____

Copyright © by Holt, Rinehart and Winston. All rights reserved.

LANGUAGE
HANDBOOK **11** WRITING EFFECTIVE SENTENCES

| WORKSHEET 5 | Combining Sentences (Rule 11 a)

EXERCISE   Combine each of the following pairs of sentences by writing one complex sentence using the subordinating conjunction *after, as, until, if,* or *because.* Add commas where necessary.

EXAMPLE   **1.** The Hubble Space Telescope has been important to astronomers.

It has provided valuable information about our solar system.

The Hubble Space Telescope has been important to astronomers _____

because it has provided valuable information about our solar system. _____

1. There are different seasons.

The earth tilts as it spins around the sun. _____

_____

_____

2. Some problems are solved.

Solar energy will heat this house. _____

_____

_____

3. You stand on the moon at night.

You can read a book by "earthlight." _____

_____

4. We saw many different constellations.

We were looking at the night sky. _____

_____

5. Scientists didn't know what was under Venus's clouds.

Space probes provided them with new information. _____

_____

_____

6. Newspapers and television showed the barren Venusian landscape.

Many space probes sent back pictures. _____

_____

_____

Copyright © by Holt, Rinehart and Winston. All rights reserved.

Continued ☞

7. A spacecraft could not land on Jupiter.

There is no solid surface on which to land. _____

_____

_____

8. Astronomers search the solar system.

They make new discoveries nearly every day. _____

_____

_____

9. Halley's comet reappeared in 1986.

Scientists discovered new information. _____

_____

_____

10. Scientists depend on pilotless space probes.

Spaceflights can take many, many years. _____

_____

_____

Copyright © by Holt, Rinehart and Winston. All rights reserved.

WORKSHEET 6 | Combining Sentences (Rule 11 a)

EXERCISE Combine each of the following pairs of sentences by writing one complex sentence using the subordinating conjunction *although, before, so that, when,* or *while.* Add commas where necessary.

EXAMPLE **1.** I toured Mexico last summer.

I saw several of Rufino Tamayo's beautiful murals.

When I toured Mexico last summer, I saw several of _____

Rufino Tamayo's beautiful murals. _____

1. Uncle Andy works in Washington, D.C.

He spends much time in Slovakia on business. _____

_____

_____

2. Julie's parents went to the sales convention.

Julie went with them. _____

_____

_____

3. Rachel decided to take the class.

She could learn Spanish. _____

_____

_____

4. They arrived at the mountain camp.

They had to climb mountains. _____

_____

_____

5. The United States is more than two hundred years old.

Many Europeans think of it as a young country. _____

_____

_____

Copyright © by Holt, Rinehart and Winston. All rights reserved.

Continued ☞

6. Jason walked up the steep streets.

He had to take deep breaths. _____

_____

_____

7. The light bulb was invented.

Homes used hundreds of candles each year. _____

_____

_____

8. We were on our way down the mountain.

Felice spotted a beautiful waterfall. _____

_____

_____

9. Tony's family visited the Anacostia Museum.

They could see many exhibits of African American history and culture. _____

_____

_____

10. Brilliant fireworks lit up the sky.

The band played "The Star-Spangled Banner." _____

_____

_____

Copyright © by Holt, Rinehart and Winston. All rights reserved.

LANGUAGE
HANDBOOK **11** **WRITING EFFECTIVE SENTENCES**

WORKSHEET 7 | **Identifying Run-on Sentences (Rule 11 b)**

EXERCISE A   On the line provided, write *S* if the sentence is correct and *R* if the sentence is a run-on sentence.

EXAMPLE   __R__   **1.** Last summer, my family and I visited Monterrey from our visit all of us gained a great appreciation for mariachi music.

_____   **1.** Our assignment was to present a "how-to" speech we decided to demonstrate origami, the Japanese art of paper folding.

_____   **2.** Why do you suppose leaves change color in the fall they certainly make the countryside pretty.

_____   **3.** How beautiful that hillside is when the aspens have all turned yellow, in the sun the hillside looks like a wall of polished gold.

_____   **4.** For a while Michael Jordan pursued a career in professional baseball then he decided to return to the Chicago Bulls to continue his great career in basketball.

_____   **5.** The lanterns swayed gently in the breeze, casting a delicate yellow light on the porch and on the buffet.

EXERCISE B   The following paragraph contains five run-on sentences. Correct each run-on sentence by adding the appropriate punctuation and capitalization.

EXAMPLE   Juanita and Daisy wanted to use their spare time constructively. ~~t~~hey discussed various projects.

Juanita has a beautiful singing voice, and Daisy plays the guitar well. The two girls decided to spend their spare time entertaining children in hospitals their hope was to lift the children's spirits. Juanita and Daisy contacted a local hospital and found that they could work as volunteers. Some of their friends became interested in the project as well the girls decided to form a group. Juanita and Daisy would perform folk songs; Bianca would do acrobatics; Theresa and Sonia would perform magic tricks. The girls rehearsed for two weeks on the day of their first show, all of the girls were somewhat nervous. There were thirty-three children in the hospital audience several doctors and nurses were also in the group. As the girls performed, they could see that the audience was enjoying the show. When the show was over, everyone, especially the children, applauded loudly, consequently, the hospital staff asked the girls to come back and perform as often as they could.

Copyright © by Holt, Rinehart and Winston. All rights reserved.

| WORKSHEET 8 | Correcting Run-on Sentences (Rule 11 b)

EXERCISE   On the line to the left of each of the following word groups, write *S* if the word group is a sentence or *R* if it is a run-on sentence. Correct each run-on sentence by making it into two separate sentences or by joining the two parts with a comma and a coordinating conjunction such as *and, but,* or *or*. Add the appropriate end marks and capital letters.

                                                                        A
EXAMPLE   __R__   **1.** Mother often says that she is "as busy as a bee." ~~after~~
                        studying the habits of bees, I now understand what the
                        expression means.

                           or

                                                                        and
                  1. Mother often says that she is "as busy as a bee," after
                        studying the habits of bees, I now understand what the
                        expression means.

_____   **1.** Have you ever read about bees how amazing they are!

_____   **2.** They are not only interesting but also useful.

_____   **3.** Bees carry pollen from one flower to another.

_____   **4.** Some farmers rent hives from professional beekeepers during the
                    blooming season, the bees help pollinate the crops.

_____   **5.** How many different kinds of bees are there they must number in the
                    thousands.

_____   **6.** We usually see only honeybees and bumblebees, occasionally we see a
                    honeycomb also.

_____   **7.** Most bees can sting at least once, stinging is the bee's method of
                    protecting itself.

_____   **8.** Bumblebees are hairy, yellow-and-black bees they are larger than most of
                    the other kinds of bees.

_____   **9.** Did you know that some bees are very selective, they collect pollen only
                    from flowers of certain families or from flowers of certain colors.

_____   **10.** Are there any books in our library about bees, I want to read more about
                    them.

Copyright © by Holt, Rinehart and Winston. All rights reserved.

| WORKSHEET 9 | **Revising Stringy Sentences and Wordy Sentences (Rule 11 c)** |

EXERCISE A   Most of the following items are stringy sentences. On the lines provided, revise each stringy sentence by (1) breaking it into two or more sentences or (2) turning some of the independent clauses into phrases or subordinate clauses. If a sentence is effective as it is, write *C*.

EXAMPLE   **1.** Clowns juggled with rings and balls, and the band played great marches, and the beautiful floats passed us.

Clowns juggled with rings and balls. The band played great marches

while the beautiful floats passed us.

1. The library was bustling with activity, and several students were talking quietly, and some were using computers, and other students were reading books and magazines.

_____

_____

2. Some Americans think that chop suey is a Chinese dish, but it is not.

_____

_____

3. Today, people live longer lives and often have more than one career.

_____

_____

4. During earliest times, observations of the sky were important in human life, and these observations are still made today, and, indeed, astronomy is likely to play an even larger part in human life in the future.

_____

_____

5. I have a book report due in English tomorrow, and I have to practice for my piano recital, and I just remembered I said I'd mow the lawn, and somehow I have to get it all done.

_____

_____

6. It seemed too quiet in the woods, and he started looking around, and he didn't see a single animal, and even the wind had died down.

_____

_____

Continued ☞

Copyright © by Holt, Rinehart and Winston. All rights reserved.

7. One day Maya hieroglyphics will be fully translated, and then we may discover the secrets of Maya masonry, and Maya history and ideas may become known.

_____

_____

8. I turned on the monitor, and I turned on the computer, and I put a floppy disk in the drive, and the lights came on, but the computer couldn't read the disk.

_____

_____

9. Chop a medium onion, and cook it in olive oil over medium heat, and wait until the onion looks transparent, and then chop three garlic cloves, and add them to the onions.

_____

_____

10. Drive north on the highway and take the third exit after the airport, and turn right, and go east for three miles, and when you see the stadium, turn right, and we're the third house on the left.

_____

_____

EXERCISE B   Most of the following sentences are wordy. On the line provided, revise each wordy sentence by (1) replacing a group of words with one word, (2) replacing a clause with a phrase, or (3) taking out a group of unnecessary words. If a sentence is effective as it is, write *C*.

> EXAMPLE **1.** In a great hurry, passengers walked to their trains.
>
> *Passengers walked hurriedly to their trains.*

1. With patience, the teacher listened to the child's story.

_____

2. They decided to reconsider the proposal that had been previously rejected.

_____

3. Because of the fact that space is limited, only fifty tickets will be sold.

_____

4. An autobiography is about the author's experiences.

_____

5. In a happy mood, the Scouts sang as they carried water to their camp in Yosemite Valley.

_____

Copyright © by Holt, Rinehart and Winston. All rights reserved.

Copyright © by Holt, Rinehart and Winston. All rights reserved.

LANGUAGE HANDBOOK 11 WRITING EFFECTIVE SENTENCES

WORKSHEET 10 | Test (Rules 11 a–c)

EXERCISE A   On the lines provided, revise the following paragraph by combining sentences.

EXAMPLE   Benita is a seventh-grader.
She attends Midland Desert Middle School.

Benita is a seventh-grader at Midland Desert Middle School.

Benita is a Navajo. She is young. She lives in a house. It is in northern New Mexico. She lives there with her family. Benita's favorite pastime is playing soccer. She often plays soccer at home with her brothers and sisters. Benita wants to play professional soccer. She practices dribbling the ball every day.

_____

_____

_____

_____

_____

_____

_____

_____

EXERCISE B   On the lines provided, revise the following paragraph by combining sentences.

EXAMPLE   Richard often goes fishing.
He often goes fishing near his home.
His home is in Chicago.

Richard often goes fishing near his home in Chicago.

Richard likes to go fishing. He fishes in Lake Michigan. For bait, he finds worms. He finds several. He finds them in the vacant lot. This lot is beside his house. He usually fishes from the pier. The pier is next to the marina. He fishes very early in the morning. His friends never catch a thing there. Richard can catch at least six fish. He can do this every time. Richard's father sometimes fishes with him. Richard's father tells stories about big catfish. The catfish are in the Mississippi River.

_____

_____

Continued ☞

_____

_____

_____

_____

_____

_____

_____

_____

EXERCISE C   The following items contain choppy, run-on, stringy, and wordy sentences. On the lines provided, revise the sentences to improve their style.

> EXAMPLE **1.** Currently, saving endangered species is a popular cause, and many people all over the world are involved in this cause, and they should continue to fight for this cause.
>
> *Currently, many people are involved in the popular cause of saving* _____
>
> *endangered species. People should continue to fight for this cause.* _____

1. Another loss is also taking place throughout the world. This loss is also great.

_____

_____

2. Some of the world's languages are dying out, stop and think for a minute about your language, and it reflects your culture and your identity.

_____

_____

3. Four hundred years ago, about 1,000 American Indian languages were spoken, but now only about 700 are spoken, and even fewer will survive in the future.

_____

_____

4. Every language expresses a unique part of the world, so language is a precious inheritance that is valuable and precious, so if you have an opportunity to learn the language of your ancestors, take it.

_____

_____

Copyright © by Holt, Rinehart and Winston. All rights reserved.

LANGUAGE HANDBOOK **12** **CAPITAL LETTERS**

WORKSHEET 1 **Using Capitals Correctly (Rules 12 a–d, g)**

EXERCISE A Proofread the following sentences for errors in capitalization. Cross out each incorrect lowercase letter and write the capital letter above it.

$$S \quad A \quad B$$
EXAMPLE 1. The largest country in ~~s~~outh ~~a~~merica is ~~b~~razil.

1. Arna Bontemps's short story "A Summer Tragedy" is set in the south.

2. their new office building is on third avenue in New york city.

3. Located in yavapai county, arizona, Tuzigoot, a national monument, features the ruins of a prehistoric pueblo.

4. The great plains is one of the world's most important wheat-growing regions.

5. My great-grandparents traveled down the ohio river on a barge.

6. during our trip to canada, my family and i stopped on cape breton island.

7. When you were in australia, did you travel in the outback?

8. our play is set in sherwood forest near nottinghamshire, england.

9. We saw mount hood in the cascade range, east of portland, oregon.

10. The geysers in yellowstone national park are a popular tourist attraction.

EXERCISE B Proofread the following sentences for errors in capitalization. Cross out each incorrect lowercase letter and write the capital letter above it.

$$D \quad C$$
EXAMPLE 1. Federico Peña was elected mayor of ~~d~~enver, ~~c~~olorado.

1. The annual shawnee ridge winter festival will begin on february 4.

2. The writer alice walker was born in eatonton, georgia, and she attended spelman college and sarah lawrence college.

3. What do the holidays fourth of july and thanksgiving day celebrate?

4. In the movie the sioux befriend the soldier they name dances with wolves.

5. The planet jupiter is about 1,300 times as large as earth.

6. Did you know that the battle of agincourt, which occurred during the middle ages, lasted only one day?

7. In 1995, Joan D. Hedrick won the pulitzer prize for her biography of harriet beecher stowe.

8. The president of the united states boarded *air force one* for a trip to beijing.

9. Eugenia w. Collier's short story "Marigolds" is set during the great depression.

10. Please be merciful and forgive us, o mighty Thor!

Copyright © by Holt, Rinehart and Winston. All rights reserved.

Elements of Literature

LANGUAGE
HANDBOOK **12** CAPITAL LETTERS

WORKSHEET 2 Using Capitals Correctly (Rules 12 b, d–f)

EXERCISE A   Proofread the following sentences for errors in capitalization. Cross out each incorrect capital or lowercase letter, and write the correct form above it.

> **EXAMPLE 1.** Recently, my sister and I̶ made plans to visit our B̶rother, who
> now lives and works on the island of H̶onshu, J̶apan.

1. I visited my sister, Arnetta, at xavier university last week.

2. She is taking several courses, including English, french, and american History.

3. After she graduates from this College, she will attend a Medical School where she will study to become a pediatrician.

4. She has applied to northwestern university in the midwest and to several schools in new York and california.

5. My brother, Luther, has already graduated from college and now teaches Mathematics classes in kyoto, japan.

6. Luther has written long, interesting letters about japanese culture.

7. Luther lives close to a buddhist temple, which he often visits with his new friends.

8. Japan's many religions include Buddhism, christianity, and shintoism.

9. Luther has also described his travels outside japan, including his trips to the gobi desert and to the mountains of tibet.

10. Arnetta and i plan to join him on his trip to bali, an island in the indian ocean.

EXERCISE B   Proofread the following sentences for errors in capitalization. Cross out each incorrect capital or lowercase letter, and write the correct form above it.

> **EXAMPLE 1.** One of the B̶alkan C̶ountries is Albania.

1. This Restaurant serves delicious cajun cuisine.

2. Aunt Anita is famous for her russian salad dressing.

3. In our study of south american countries, we learned about peruvian customs, venezuelan oil fields, and brazilian Rain Forests.

4. Do you know the first three letters of the greek alphabet?

5. The israeli ambassador met with european leaders to discuss a new Trade Agreement.

Copyright © by Holt, Rinehart and Winston. All rights reserved.

LANGUAGE HANDBOOK	**12**	CAPITAL LETTERS

WORKSHEET 3 **Capitalizing Proper Nouns (Rule 12 d)**

EXERCISE A   On the line provided, write the letter of the noun that is correctly capitalized.

EXAMPLE ___b___ **1.** (a) united Parcel Service   (b) United Parcel Service

_____ **1.** (a) Better Business Bureau   (b) Better Business bureau

_____ **2.** (a) Statue of Liberty   (b) statue of Liberty

_____ **3.** (a) asian americans   (b) Asian Americans

_____ **4.** (a) Bethune-Cookman College   (b) Bethune-Cookman college

_____ **5.** (a) a High School student   (b) a high school student

_____ **6.** (a) United Airlines   (b) united airlines

_____ **7.** (a) Wake Island   (b) Wake island

_____ **8.** (a) Cannes film festival   (b) Cannes Film Festival

_____ **9.** (a) Mississippi River   (b) Mississippi river

_____ **10.** (a) the Apollo Theater   (b) the Apollo theater

EXERCISE B   Proofread the following sentences for errors in capitalization. Cross out each incorrect capital letter or lowercase letter, and write the correct form above it.

EXAMPLE **1.** A Salvation Army Truck pulled up in front of our house.

1. There is a fine University in our town, but Maya's brother wants to attend Morehouse college in atlanta, georgia.

2. The Lodge's full name is the Benevolent and protective order of Elks of the U.S.A.

3. The National Association For The Advancement Of Colored People (NAACP) was founded in 1909.

4. This Book by Sonia Sanchez was published by Africa world press, inc.

5. Langston has a savings account at the first national bank of chicago.

6. The chicago bulls have won several national basketball association Championship Titles.

7. Some of eric's friends gave up Desserts for lent.

8. The federal express Delivery Person picked up Heather's package that had to be in Dallas by the Next Day.

9. Did you see the washington monument when you were in washington, d.c.?

10. In 1958, the *nautilus* became the first Submarine to sail under the ice at the north pole.

Copyright © by Holt, Rinehart and Winston. All rights reserved.

LANGUAGE HANDBOOK **12** CAPITAL LETTERS

WORKSHEET 4 **Capitalizing Titles (Rule 12 g)**

EXERCISE A   Capitalize the following titles according to the capitalization rules in your textbook. Cross out each incorrect lowercase letter, and write the capital letter above it.

$$\overset{C}{}\qquad\overset{T}{}$$

EXAMPLE **1.** the ~~c~~hicago ~~t~~ribune

1. *daughter of the mountains*

2. the *cherokee phoenix*

3. the *musical quarterly*

4. *crossing the bridge*

5. the *buenos aires herald*

6. "the bells of santa cruz"

7. the *texas monthly*

8. *the house on mango street*

9. *their eyes were watching god*

10. "the song of the smoke"

11. *everybody loves raymond*

12. bill of rights

13. *beauty and the beast*

14. *saved by the bell*

15. "the flying tortilla man"

16. *national geographic*

17. *better homes and gardens*

18. "how do i live?"

19. *the marriage of figaro*

20. *fences* by August Wilson

EXERCISE B   Proofread the following sentences for errors in capitalization. Cross out each incorrect capital or lowercase letter, and write the correct form above it.

$$\overset{G}{}\qquad\qquad\overset{P}{}$$

EXAMPLE **1.** Most people supported ~~g~~overnor Bush's ~~p~~roposal.

1. My mother has just been made President of her company.

2. Indeed, aunt mabel told me she subscribed to *ebony*.

3. We were interviewed by a Reporter from the *hillside news*.

4. The president left the white house for a vacation at Camp David.

5. The singing was led by colonel Gutiérrez of the Marine Corps.

6. When grandmother Kostas comes to visit, she always brings presents.

7. Nora Ephron has written books titled *crazy salad* and *scribble, scribble*.

8. The Captain of the ship, Lieutenant Homer Creech, received a personal letter from secretary of the navy Smith.

9. Did you say, Uncle, that you have not read Ron Arias's book *five against the sea*?

10. After dinner, mother read aloud from a translation of *Snow White and the seven dwarfs*.

Copyright © by Holt, Rinehart and Winston. All rights reserved.

Elements of Literature

LANGUAGE HANDBOOK **12** CAPITAL LETTERS

WORKSHEET 5 Test (Rules 12 a–g)

EXERCISE A   Proofread the following sentences for errors in capitalization. Cross out each incorrect lowercase letter, and write the capital letter above it.

>   *A*   *L*   *N*   *B*
> **EXAMPLE 1.** Ms. A̸beyto is a vice president of the L̸incoln N̸ational B̸ank.

1. Has Audrey joined the american renaissance literary club?

2. the employees of the good morning breakfast cereal company held their banquet at the metropolitan hotel.

3. The members of the explorers club from diego ribas middle school are making plans for a camping trip along the rio grande.

4. The battle of gettysburg continued through July 3, 1863.

5. one of the major holidays in judaism is rosh hashana.

6. Among the religions practiced in india are buddhism, hinduism, and christianity.

7. The canadians have a national holiday called canada day, which they celebrate on the first day of july.

8. Two of bella's favorite foods are french toast and new england clam chowder.

9. Besides italy, can you name another mediterranean country?

10. the latin name for the greek goddess aphrodite is venus.

11. last spring, my family and i visited washington, d.c., where we saw the vietnam veterans memorial and other national monuments.

12. Of mercury, venus, mars, and earth, which planet is closest to the sun?

13. in 1927, charles lindbergh flew the airplane *spirit of st. louis* nonstop from new york city to paris.

14. Of the dallas cowboys, the buffalo bills, and the pittsburgh steelers, which football team has played in the most super bowl games?

15. Is sardinia the name of the largest island directly south of the french island of corsica?

16. In egyptian mythology the sun god and principal deity is ra.

17. Please ease our sorrows, o beautiful Apollo!

18. In my american history class, I learned about the history, culture, and language of the cherokee nation.

19. This newsmagazine features a profile of secretary of state madeleine albright.

20. My aunt was a peace corps volunteer in north africa.

Continued ☞

Copyright © by Holt, Rinehart and Winston. All rights reserved.

EXERCISE B   Proofread the following sentences for errors in capitalization. Cross out each incorrect capital or lowercase letter, and write the correct form above it.

EXAMPLE   **1.** The C̷ommander of the ship *Pequod* is C̷aptain Ahab.

1. My Uncle has written a book called *Everyday weather for you*.

2. Becky has a summer job working for the newspaper *norwich bugle*.

3. I saw the story about commander kay in the *wisconsin alumni Bulletin*.

4. We subscribe to the sunday edition of *The New york times*, and it always arrives early Sunday Morning.

5. Jacqueline says her favorite animal story is *ring of bright water*, but I like *the call of the wild* much better.

6. I can identify with the young narrator of Gary Soto's short story "the jacket."

7. Rafe Buenrostro is the main character of Rolando Hinojosa-Smith's novel *fair gentlemen of belken county*.

8. President Abraham Lincoln wrote five different versions of the gettysburg address, a Speech he gave during the civil war.

9. Latoya, my oldest Sister, played the part of Berniece in our school's production of August Wilson's play *the piano lesson*.

10. My Aunt Aretha gave me a print of *the banjo lesson*, an oil painting by Henry Ossawa Tanner.

EXERCISE C   Proofread the following paragraph for errors in capitalization. Cross out each incorrect capital or lowercase letter, and write the correct form above it.

EXAMPLE   **[1]** T̷he P̷anama C̷anal is a great E̷ngineering accomplishment.

[1] linking the Atlantic ocean with the Pacific ocean, the Panama canal took ten years and approximately $380 Million to build. [2] two french firms and one from the United States gave up before the United States completed the project in 1914. [3] more than 43,000 workers faced jungles, swamps, volcanic earth, Malaria, and Yellow fever. [4] when it was completed, the Canal cut about 8,000 miles from a ship's journey from New York to san francisco. [5] today, the Canal is important to both commercial Trade and Defense of the United States, as 12,500 ships travel through the Canal's Locks every year.

Copyright © by Holt, Rinehart and Winston. All rights reserved.

Elements of Literature

WORKSHEET 1 Using End Marks (Rules 13 a–e)

EXERCISE A For each of the following sentences, insert the correct end mark.

EXAMPLE 1. May I take a message**?**

1. Have you ever heard Yo-Yo Ma's music

2. Larry, why are spiders not classified as insects

3. What a fabulous story you have told

4. Yes, Sitting Bull was a medicine man and leader of the Hunkpapa Sioux

5. Look at those shooting stars

6. Write your last name first and your first name last

7. How do the Laplanders' lives and those of the reindeer intertwine

8. How lucky you were to see whales

9. These tiny South American frogs are brilliantly colored

10. Where did you get that old guitar

EXERCISE B For each of the following sentences, insert periods, question marks, and exclamation points where they are needed.

EXAMPLE 1. Do you know how to get to the post office at 402 Main St.**?**

1. My science class begins at 2:30 PM, and the lab for that class ends at 4:00 PM

2. We know author William Sydney Porter by his pen name, O Henry

3. My aunt rode the train from Chicago, Ill, to Denver, Colo, when she came to visit us in Boulder

4. Dr David Livingstone was the first non-African to cross Africa from west to east

5. When will Mr and Mrs Belindo return from their vacation in Nashville, Tenn

6. Oops When I mailed in my order for the model rocket kit, I mistakenly addressed it to P O Box 411 instead of to P O Box 114

7. Have you ever made mistakes in which you transposed numbers or letters

8. Hurry Our plane leaves for Orlando, Fla, at 4:10 PM, which is only thirty minutes from now

9. We will be staying with Mr and Mrs H L Robinson, Jr, who are friends of our family

10. Mr Robinson works in the Municipal Justice Bldg, and Mrs. Robinson works for Univacuum, Inc, as a salesperson

Copyright © by Holt, Rinehart and Winston. All rights reserved.

LANGUAGE
HANDBOOK **13** **PUNCTUATION**

WORKSHEET 2 | Using Commas in a Series (Rules 13 f, g)

EXERCISE A   Insert commas where they belong in the following sentences. If a sentence is correct without commas, write *C* on the line provided.

> EXAMPLE _____ 1. This magazine features articles about the leaders Nelson Mandela, Benjamin Netanyahu, and Ernesto Zedillo.

_____ 1. Fishing snow skiing and scuba diving are my favorite sports.

_____ 2. They wanted to ride horses go hiking and explore the cave.

_____ 3. Our reading list includes books by Gary Soto Julia Alvarez and Amy Tan.

_____ 4. The four principal islands of Japan are Honshu Shikoku Kyushu and Hokkaido.

_____ 5. Photographers reporters and tourists got off the plane.

_____ 6. An infestation of insects damaged crops chewed lawns and harmed fruit trees.

_____ 7. Something flashed and sparkled and darted across the sky.

_____ 8. The grass trees and flowers glowed in the evening light.

_____ 9. We had a telephone electricity and even hot water in our cabin.

_____ 10. This restaurant serves breakfast lunch and dinner.

_____ 11. The engineer admired the smooth workings of the large complex shiny gears in the machinery.

_____ 12. The man had a long narrow and sad face.

_____ 13. Her floor was covered with bright colorful balloons twisted into fanciful hats and delightful animals.

_____ 14. I need pineapple and carrots and bananas for the salad.

_____ 15. Mom eats lunch in a restaurant in the park or sometimes at her desk.

_____ 16. We recently studied the Maya Aztec and Inca civilizations.

_____ 17. Iris wanted to be a lawyer an employment counselor or a teacher.

_____ 18. We need to warm the pita bread slice the tomatoes and wash the lettuce before we make the sandwiches for our picnic.

_____ 19. Mrs. Lewis told the baby sitter where she would be how to contact her and when she would return.

_____ 20. In the room, Ossie had mixed stripes with plaids combined polka dots with a paisley pattern and added curtains with ruffles.

Copyright © by Holt, Rinehart and Winston. All rights reserved.

LANGUAGE
HANDBOOK **13 PUNCTUATION**

WORKSHEET 3 | **Using Commas in Compound Sentences (Rule 13 h)**

EXERCISE A Add commas where they belong in the following sentences.

EXAMPLE **1.** Snakes cannot hear very well**,** but their bodies are quite sensitive to the movements of others.

1. Snakes are both legless and armless yet muscles attached to movable ribs allow them to swim and crawl.

2. All snakes have forked tongues and they use their tongues to smell their prey.

3. Snakes can raise their body temperature by lying on a rock in the sun and they can cool themselves by seeking shade.

4. Rattlesnakes do not always rattle before striking so you should not expect this warning sign.

5. You can determine the age of a tree by the number of its rings but you cannot tell the age of a rattlesnake by the number of its rattles.

6. A rattlesnake usually gains a new rattle after shedding its skin so it may gain two to four rattles a year.

7. A rattlesnake usually does not have more than ten rattles for additional rattles often fall off.

8. Cobras can form a hood by expanding the movable ribs behind the head and these snakes often do so when they are ready to strike.

9. People may fear snakes because of superstition or they may fear snakes because some species are poisonous.

10. Some countries are free of snakes but the United States is not one of them.

EXERCISE B Insert commas where they belong in the following sentences.

EXAMPLE **1.** The giant statues of Easter Island were first seen by Europeans in 1722**,** and the statues still have an air of mystery.

1. The figures were carved hundreds of years ago from volcanic rock on one side of the island and then they were moved to other locations on the island.

2. Most of the statues are between eleven and twenty feet tall but others stand forty feet high.

3. Observers suggest ways the people of Easter Island might have moved these huge statues yet no one has provided a good explanation.

4. One legend is that the statues walked across the island themselves but this story is clearly fanciful.

5. No one knows all the facts about the statues so the mystery surrounding them continues.

Copyright © by Holt, Rinehart and Winston. All rights reserved.

LANGUAGE
HANDBOOK **13** PUNCTUATION

WORKSHEET 4 | Using Commas with Interrupters (Rule 13 i)

EXERCISE   Most of the following sentences contain nonessential phrases or clauses. Add commas where they are needed. If a sentence is correct, write *C*.

EXAMPLE _____ 1. The crowd, seeing Tyrone on his feet, broke into applause.

_____ 1. Geronimo who led the Chiricahua Apaches was a great leader.

_____ 2. The salad that she made for the potluck dinner was a colorful mix of tomatoes, artichoke hearts, carrots, and black olives.

_____ 3. Hercules whose picture can be found on many ancient Greek pottery pieces was the son of Zeus.

_____ 4. In Mexico City, a man hoping for a sale wore hats stacked one on the other.

_____ 5. Why is it do you think that she always slept with the doll lying by her side?

_____ 6. The bride Satori who was from Osaka chose a traditional wedding garment.

_____ 7. That new ad you saw which appeared in this morning's paper is bringing in many new customers.

_____ 8. Have I introduced you to Mr. Perkins our kind and generous neighbor?

_____ 9. Ms. Ortega who was our teacher last year will teach at Adams Middle School next year.

_____ 10. This bronze statue cast in over a dozen pieces will be put together next month.

_____ 11. Do you think that the audience excited by the show will give the performers a standing ovation?

_____ 12. A goal even if it is small is best approached in stages.

_____ 13. That last Easter egg carefully placed by Rudy certainly is well hidden.

_____ 14. Pocahontas's story which has been told for over three hundred years sometimes strays from the facts.

_____ 15. We met the woman who will be the violin soloist with the orchestra.

_____ 16. Will this new information learned only an hour ago interest the voters?

_____ 17. Lonnie dreaming of flying in a spacecraft stared up at the stars.

_____ 18. The house's owners who like to do such work themselves are painting.

_____ 19. All the animals shown on the facing page are expert swimmers and divers.

_____ 20. These ancient Chinese tombs discovered only a few years ago are still being excavated.

Copyright © by Holt, Rinehart and Winston. All rights reserved.

WORKSHEET 5 | Using Commas with Interrupters and Introductory Elements (Rules 13 i, j)

EXERCISE A   Insert commas where they are necessary in the following sentences.

> **EXAMPLE 1.** My mother, I think, is preparing vegetable soup for dinner.

1. How many gold medals did Carl Lewis who was an Olympic sprinter and long jumper win?

2. Alfre Woodard in my opinion deserved the award.

3. Will you Angelica return my book when you go to the library?

4. Ireland the Emerald Isle lies west of Britain.

5. In fact Octavio Paz won the Nobel Prize in literature in 1990.

6. Just at twilight the finest hour of the day the moon rose.

7. The auditorium was a gift of Henry Allerdyce the financier.

8. He speaks I believe the truth.

9. Constance Whitman the helicopter pilot promised to be there.

10. I told them on the contrary that my twin brother Eric is a salesperson.

EXERCISE B   Insert commas where they are necessary in the following sentences.

> **EXAMPLE 1.** Edythe White, my neighbor, reminds me of Oprah Winfrey.

1. Edythe a talented performer longs to act on a Broadway stage.

2. In my opinion she will soon be performing there.

3. She studies acting with Reynold Williams the famous director at a theater workshop where he teaches.

4. When an acting school is connected to a theater it is called a theater workshop.

5. Yes students can try out for roles in theater performances.

6. Edythe will audition no doubt for one of the roles in a summer production of August Wilson's *The Piano Lesson*.

7. In fact the director has told her that she has an excellent chance of getting a part.

8. Indeed Edythe can sing and dance as well as act.

9. To tell the truth you would say that she comes alive when on stage.

10. In the summer after high school graduation Edythe would like to work in a New York theater.

Copyright © by Holt, Rinehart and Winston. All rights reserved.

LANGUAGE HANDBOOK **13** **PUNCTUATION**

WORKSHEET 6

Using Commas in Conventional Situations
(Rule 13 k)

EXERCISE A   Insert the necessary commas in the following sentences.

EXAMPLE **1.** The return address is 631 Chatham Lane, Houston, Texas 77027.

1. On Wednesday January 21 1998 Pope John Paul II traveled to Havana Cuba.

2. My friend is traveling here from Providence Rhode Island.

3. Enrique lives at 287 Austin Street Duluth Minnesota 55803.

4. Since Friday August 13 1999 Jiro has been taking piano lessons.

5. Mail the letter to 25 Foster Lane Billings Montana 59102.

6. Darlene used to live at 1002 Carson Avenue Baltimore Maryland 21224.

7. Martin Luther King, Jr., was born on January 15 1929 in Atlanta Georgia.

8. Relatives are flying here from San Juan Puerto Rico.

9. On our way to Mexico, we stopped in Houston Texas.

10. The address given in the letter is Room 2930 52 Whitney Way Erie PA 16511.

EXERCISE B   Insert the necessary commas in the following sentences. If a sentence is punctuated correctly, write *C* on the line provided.

EXAMPLE _____ **1.** The president of the United States resides at 1600 Pennsylvania Avenue, Washington, D.C.

_____ **1.** This letter was sent from 18 Grassmere Avenue Flint Michigan 48504.

_____ **2.** Selena also visited friends in Dallas and Midland.

_____ **3.** On October 1 1847 Maria Mitchell discovered a new comet.

_____ **4.** World War II ended on September 2 1945.

_____ **5.** Stacy Kempner moved from East Brunswick New Jersey to Boulder Colorado.

_____ **6.** On June 1 1937 Amelia Earhart started out on her final flight from Miami Florida.

_____ **7.** My cousin, Mary Lee, lives in Rome New York not in Rome Georgia.

_____ **8.** Abigail Adams died on October 18 1818.

_____ **9.** Tony's address is 194 Foothill Drive Ogden Utah 84403.

_____ **10.** The Leonards sailed on Friday November 5 1999 for a trip to the Philippines.

Copyright © by Holt, Rinehart and Winston. All rights reserved.

LANGUAGE
HANDBOOK **13** **PUNCTUATION**

WORSHEET 7 | **Using Commas, Semicolons, and Colons**
(Rules 13 k–n)

EXERCISE A   The following numbered items contain errors in the use of commas, semicolons, or colons. Add, delete, or change punctuation as needed.

EXAMPLE   [1] Here's a letter from Hank; let's read it now.

[1] Dear Classmates

  [2] Well, I finally made it to my aunt's ranch outside of Melbourne Australia. [3] We arrived at 2 30 A.M. the day before yesterday. [4] Life on a sheep ranch certainly is different than life in town, for starters, we get up at 5 00 A.M.! [5] In just two days, I have seen the following sights kangaroos, a dingo, emus, and miles and miles of grassland. [6] I spend most of my time with my cousins, who are taking care of the sheep, tomorrow we are going to a neighboring ranch to help with sheepshearing. [7] By the way they call sheep "woollybacks" here. [8] Please send me these things a picture of the class, a list of everyone's addresses, and lots and lots of letters. [9] Well, the mail leaves at 3 15, and that gives me about five minutes, so I'll say so long for now.

[10] Your friend

Hank

EXERCISE B   Most of the following sentences contain at least one error in the use of semicolons or colons. On the line provided, write each word or number that should be followed by a semicolon or colon, adding the correct punctuation. If a sentence is correct, write *C*.

EXAMPLE   _4:00_   **1.** Shall we begin at 4 00?

_____   **1.** At noon, the monkeys sat in the shade of the leafy treetops, some napped, while others groomed each other.

_____   **2.** Customs were very different then today people rarely wear gloves in the summer.

_____   **3.** Some reliable bulbs for beginning gardeners include tulips, daffodils, and gladioluses.

_____   **4.** The movie will be over by 8 40 then we'll come right home.

_____   **5.** The following students should report to the gym immediately Jason, Vera, Dorothy, and T. J.

Continued ☞

Copyright © by Holt, Rinehart and Winston. All rights reserved.

LANGUAGE HANDBOOK **13** **WORKSHEET 7** *(continued)*

EXERCISE C   Insert the necessary commas in the following sentences. If a sentence is punctuated correctly, write *C* on the line provided.

> **EXAMPLE** _____ **1.** *Apollo 11*'s lunar module landed on the moon on July 20, 1969.

_____ **1.** Next week we hope to visit the cliff-dweller ruins in Tonto County Arizona.

_____ **2.** The wedding took place on Monday December 28 1998 at 2:00 P.M.

_____ **3.** Melba has just returned from a trip to Paris France.

_____ **4.** Until January 3 2000 my home was on Michigan Boulevard in Chicago.

_____ **5.** These pictures were taken last month at Lake George New York.

_____ **6.** *Old Ironsides* was launched on October 21 1797.

_____ **7.** Elizabeth Barrett lived at 50 Wimpole Street London England.

_____ **8.** On September 12 1846 she married Robert Browning.

_____ **9.** It took Narcissa Whitman about five months to travel from Missouri to the Columbia River in 1836.

_____ **10.** Gwendolyn Brooks was born in 1917 and has lived for most of her life in Chicago Illinois.

EXERCISE D   Insert the necessary commas in the following letter.

> **EXAMPLE** [1] I was born on November 16, 1988, at 2:00 P.M.

[1] Dear Aunt Lois

[2] I was so happy to hear from you on Thursday November 16. [3] My birthday was a really special day because you and two of my friends from Chicago Illinois called me. [4] Your gift to me is so wonderful—airline tickets to visit you in Orlando Florida! [5] We have a two-week break from school starting December 15 2000. [6] I will be on the plane Saturday December 16. [7] I am pleased that I don't have to transfer airplanes in Atlanta Georgia. [8] Will my cousin Larry be home from school in Miami Florida? [9] I can't wait to leave the cold, wet weather here in Cincinnati Ohio and see you in sunny Florida.

[10] Your loving nephew

Brandon

Copyright © by Holt, Rinehart and Winston. All rights reserved.

Elements of Literature

LANGUAGE HANDBOOK **13** **PUNCTUATION**

WORKSHEET 8 | Test (Rules 13 a–n)

EXERCISE A The following sentences contain errors in the use of end marks, semicolons, or colons. Insert appropriate punctuation where it is needed.

EXAMPLE 1. What is your P.O. Box number**?**

1. Nelson Mandela spent many years as a political prisoner before being elected South Africa's first black president

2. Be at the airport an hour ahead of time; your plane leaves at 8 30 sharp.

3. What great philosopher died around 347 B.C.

4. Oh, no, we're late

5. Foods that originated in the Americas include the following corn, squash, and chocolate.

6. What is the meaning of *meridiem,* on which the abbreviations AM and PM are based?

7. The Scouts are camping out at the lake they camp there every summer.

8. Did Dr. Livingstone ever find the source of the Congo River

9. Point out Lima, Peru, on the map

10. Mr and Mrs Waters have opened a new shop; it's on Jackson Street.

EXERCISE B Insert commas where they are necessary in the following sentences.

EXAMPLE 1. During her senior year, Janell's address was East Hall**,** 203 Milnor Avenue**,** Buffalo**,** New York 14218.

1. The chief crops grown in India include rice coffee and cotton.

2. Small colorful shrill birds flew across the field.

3. We bought fresh tomatoes jalapeño peppers green bell peppers and onions and made our own salsa.

4. The reporter interviewed the mayor wrote the article and then typed it.

5. For example your voice was too soft at the beginning.

6. I still say however that she should have tried harder.

7. The nation's economy we think will improve.

8. Citlaltepetl a volcano is the highest peak in Mexico.

9. All records for dates prior to January 23 1907 were destroyed in the fire of November 13 1919 that burned down the city hall.

10. We're selling the building at 17 Lamar Drive Kansas City Missouri.

Continued ☞

Copyright © by Holt, Rinehart and Winston. All rights reserved.

EXERCISE C   Insert the commas that are missing from the following sentences. If a sentence is punctuated correctly, write *C* on the line provided.

EXAMPLE _____ 1. Who are Robert Wadlow, Albert Kramer, and Jane Bunford?

_____ 1. You are no doubt used to hearing about basketball centers football ends and baseball pitchers who are more than six feet six inches tall.

_____ 2. Indeed the basketball star Hakeem Olajuwon is seven feet tall.

_____ 3. Olajuwon however would look rather small beside either Robert Pershing Wadlow or Albert Johann Kramer.

_____ 4. Kramer a man from the Netherlands is officially listed as eight feet four inches tall and Wadlow attained a height of eight feet eleven inches.

_____ 5. Wadlow's greatest recorded weight was 491 pounds but he weighed only 439 pounds at the time of his death.

_____ 6. Wadlow the tallest person in medical history died on July 15 1940 in Manistee Michigan.

_____ 7. Measuring seven feet nine inches Jane Bunford was the tallest woman of her time.

_____ 8. She was born on July 26 1895 and lived near Birmingham England.

_____ 9. Sandy Allen born in Chicago Illinois was seven feet one inch tall at the age of sixteen and today she measures seven feet seven inches.

_____ 10. The tallest woman in history however was Zeng Jinlian of China.

_____ 11. Circuses have often claimed to have performers eight or nine feet tall but these claims do not hold up.

_____ 12. These performers in fact are usually under contract not to be measured.

_____ 13. No circus performer has ever been found to be taller than Wadlow Kramer or Bunford.

_____ 14. One circus for example claimed the "World's Tallest Man" of nine feet six inches but he was found to be under seven feet four inches.

_____ 15. Why even respectable scientists get carried away with this game of claims.

_____ 16. In 1872, anthropologists biologists and doctors believed that Daniel Cajanus a Finn was nine feet three and a half inches tall and the tallest man who ever lived.

_____ 17. When his bones were dug up they measured two feet less.

_____ 18. Haji Mohammed Alam Channa a man from Pakistan was born in 1953.

_____ 19. He was reported to have attained the height of eight feet three inches.

_____ 20. When he was measured in New York in 1987 however his height was only seven feet eight inches.

Copyright © by Holt, Rinehart and Winston. All rights reserved.

Elements of Literature

Copyright © by Holt, Rinehart and Winston. All rights reserved.

LANGUAGE HANDBOOK 14 PUNCTUATION

WORKSHEET 1 Using Underlining (Italics) (Rules 14 a, b)

EXERCISE In each of the following sentences, underline each word, letter, or figure that should be italicized.

> **EXAMPLE 1.** Yes, s's can and should be used in letters involving money.

1. Harry and the Hendersons is a film about people who meet a friendly Bigfoot.

2. For many years, mystery surrounded the sinking of the battleship Maine.

3. You don't need six !'s here; one will do nicely.

4. I didn't know that the film The Wizard of Oz was based on a book.

5. Have you read the novel The Cay by Theodore Taylor?

6. How many i's are in the word Mississippi?

7. The Orient Express, one of the most famous trains in Europe, operated between Paris, France, and Istanbul, Turkey.

8. Did you know that cities are visible at night from the space shuttle Endeavour?

9. Since he loves the program so much, I wouldn't bother him while he's watching a rerun of Bill Nye the Science Guy.

10. Did you see the article on Nairobi in Newsweek magazine?

11. What was that wonderful song at the beginning of the movie Fly Away Home?

12. The composer Mozart was Austrian, but the lyrics for his opera The Marriage of Figaro are in Italian.

13. Was the musical Annie performed on Broadway?

14. An excellent source of information on the Congo River is a book called The River Congo by Peter Forbath.

15. Try to limit the number of really's you use when you speak.

16. Was the huge, wooden airplane known as the Spruce Goose ever put to practical use?

17. Both children and adults enjoy listening to a recording of Peter and the Wolf, a symphonic fairy tale.

18. This issue of National Geographic examines a few interesting insects such as the bumble bee and the cicada.

19. Van Gogh painted ordinary household objects in several of his works, such as the painting Van Gogh's Chair.

20. Some people put a line through the middle of their 7's so that the numbers won't be confused with 1's.

LANGUAGE HANDBOOK **14** PUNCTUATION

| WORKSHEET 2 | Using Quotation Marks (Rules 14 c–h)

EXERCISE A   Add capital letters, periods, question marks, commas, and quotation marks where they are needed for the direct quotations in the following sentences.

> EXAMPLE 1. " _L_ let's talk to the superintendent of our building **,"** Mandy said to Brenda.

1. We would like to plant a roof garden Mandy said.

2. That sounds like a good idea the superintendent replied.

3. Brenda asked could we use a small section of the roof on the south side

4. Aretha added we really wouldn't need too much space

5. I'm certain something could be arranged commented the superintendent.

6. Then he added what are you planning to grow

7. We were thinking of growing tomatoes, lettuce, strawberries, and daisies Mandy replied.

8. Brenda said I was planning also to set aside a tiny section for herbs

9. I'll help you block off a small section this afternoon the superintendent responded.

10. The friends cheerfully replied oh, thank you very much

EXERCISE B   Add punctuation marks and capital letters where they are needed in the following sentences.

> EXAMPLE 1. Arlena asked, " _H_ has anyone seen Coach Terada?**"**

1. Where's Arlena asked Coach Terada. I want to congratulate her.

2. Here I am! shouted Arlena.

3. Congratulations, Arlena! exclaimed the coach. I knew you would win!

4. Arlena asked how did you know?

5. The coach explained you have all of the qualities of a champion.

6. What do you mean Arlena asked.

7. Well, you're an extremely talented tennis player said Coach Terada but perhaps even more important is that you have a great deal of determination and persistence.

8. Well, I will admit said Arlena that I do practice hard every day.

9. I know you do said the coach. I'm very proud of you, Arlena.

10. Thanks, Coach Arlena said.

Copyright © by Holt, Rinehart and Winston. All rights reserved.

WORKSHEET 3 | Using Quotation Marks (Rules 14 c–l)

EXERCISE A   Add commas and quotation marks where they are needed in the following sentences.

> **EXAMPLE 1.** "I wonder," Jenny said, "when the tickets for the concert will go on sale."

1. Louis Braille was a teacher in France who created the Braille writing system, said Ms. O'Hara.

2. The caption says, A Bhutanese monastery, or *dzong*, Tess reported.

3. Carmen said This week I am reading *Fifth Chinese Daughter* by Jade Snow Wong.

4. Have a look at the article called Saving Our Parks in last Sunday's paper.

5. Trust me the scout whispered and I'll lead you safely out of this cavern.

6. In this region of Ireland said Mr. O'Hare we grow potatoes, oats, and wheat.

7. Julia said I think I would have liked traveling in a covered wagon.

8. Can you explain the title of Amy Tan's story Fish Cheeks?

9. My dad said, In chess, knights are the only pieces that can jump over pieces in their path, Bill explained.

10. Mr. Hill continued, Fold the paper in half. Then, fold it in half again. Take the scissors and cut a triangle out of the folded corner. Then, unfold the paper.

EXERCISE B   Add commas and quotation marks where they are needed in the following dialogue. Insert the paragraph sign (¶) to show where the speaker changes and a new paragraph should begin.

> **EXAMPLE** ¶ Cheryl said to Racquel, "The first issue of the school newspaper will be printed on Friday."

Racquel, have you developed the photographs for the school paper yet? asked Cheryl. We need them by noon. "Yes said Racquel. I took them to Mrs. Ortega's office. Cheryl inquired "How did they turn out? Was the lighting good enough? I had some difficulty with the three shots I took at night Racquel responded, but the rest are pretty sharp. That's great! said Cheryl. After all our hard work, I almost can't wait to see the first issue of the paper.

Copyright © by Holt, Rinehart and Winston. All rights reserved.

LANGUAGE
HANDBOOK **14** PUNCTUATION

| WORKSHEET 4 | Test (Rules 14 a–l)

EXERCISE A   Each of the following sentences contains at least one item that should be either underlined (to indicate italics) or placed in quotation marks. Insert the proper punctuation for each item.

EXAMPLE **1.** Is this word <u>cat</u> or <u>vat</u>?

1. Every parent in the audience beamed as the seventh-graders sang High Hopes.

2. Avoid overusing the conjunction so.

3. Ernesto Galarza's nonfiction book Barrio Boy made me want to write a book about my own life.

4. What does the expression "Mind your p's and q's" mean?

5. It's a Wonderful Life is on television tonight; this will make the twelfth time Mom has seen that movie.

6. I'm calling my poem Ode to a Toad.

7. How many 0's are in one trillion?

8. Hundreds of issues of Scientific American were stacked neatly in the attic.

9. How much of Gary Soto's story The No-Guitar Blues is based on real events?

10. Seeing Monet's Water Lilies in person is definitely better than seeing a photograph of the painting.

EXERCISE B   Add punctuation marks where they are needed in the following sentences.

EXAMPLE **1.** Han asked**,** **"** In Norse mythology, is Odin the name of the chief god**?"**

1. Your resistance to my plan he said is understandable.

2. I'm so eager to go to Florida she said that I can hardly wait.

3. Ms. Beame asked Is Mount Aconcagua the highest peak in the Andes?

4. This summer we are going on vacation to the mountain states. First, we're driving to Colorado to see Pikes Peak and Mount Elbert. Then, we're going to see the Teton Range, and, finally, we're camping at Yellowstone National Park, Corey told us.

5. Cindy asked, Do you know the words to that song that starts, You've got to walk that lonesome valley?

6. What I want to know she said is how you want to celebrate your birthday.

7. Did Mr. Parks receive the Congressional Medal of Honor she asked.

8. You studied hard he said and that's why you did so well.

Continued ☞

Copyright © by Holt, Rinehart and Winston. All rights reserved.

Elements of Literature

9. Where did you find the article Raising Ladybugs, Ramon? asked Mr. Jones.

10. The chapter called Proper Nutrition and You, has an excellent illustration of the food pyramid.

EXERCISE C   Add the commas, quotation marks, and capital letters needed in the following dialogue. Insert the paragraph sign (¶) to show where each new paragraph should begin.

> EXAMPLE ¶ " ⎯You're supposed to be in your bed asleep," said Charlotte's mother.

Mom said Charlotte plaintively I'm certain I heard a noise like the opening of a spaceship's air lock. well, that's quite an imagination you have, Charlotte her mother replied. I think it's in the back yard the girl continued. that's just fine murmured the girl's mother. The young girl's voice sank to a frightened whisper as she said please, Mom, we've got to do something. They're coming out. They've turned on their ray guns. I think they're Martians. Quick! lock the door! aren't you listening, Mom? I can't hear what you're saying her mother responded. How can you just sit there at a time like this? the girl shouted. Wearily, Charlotte's mother said, just a minute, dear, I must see who's at our front door. No, Mom, don't! Charlotte screamed as she suddenly awoke and sat up in her bed.

EXERCISE D   On the lines provided, use the abbreviations *DQ* or *IQ* to identify each of the following sentences as a direct quotation or an indirect quotation. Then, add quotation marks where they are needed, and circle letters that should be capitalized.

> EXAMPLE __DQ__ 1. Mrs. Jennings asked, "do you think you can baby-sit Todd Saturday night?"

_____ 1. I told her that I had another job baby-sitting another child that night.

_____ 2. When I got home, my father said, Mr. Lambert called to say that little Leslie has a cold, so you won't be sitting with her this Saturday.

_____ 3. Hello, Mrs. Jennings, I said. have you found another sitter for Saturday night?

_____ 4. I had often said that Todd was an enjoyable child.

_____ 5. She exclaimed, oh, I'm so glad you called! We could not find anyone else who could work Saturday.

Copyright © by Holt, Rinehart and Winston. All rights reserved.

LANGUAGE
HANDBOOK **15** PUNCTUATION

WORKSHEET 1 | **Using Apostrophes (Rule 15 a)**

EXERCISE On the line provided, correctly write and punctuate each of the following word groups to show possession.

EXAMPLES 1. the clerk computer _____*the clerk's computer*_____

2. the Johnsons house _____*the Johnsons' house*_____

1. the geese wings _____

2. some person job _____

3. the rainbow colors _____

4. Perseus sword _____

5. the moon orbit _____

6. some books titles _____

7. the ships flags _____

8. our players uniforms _____

9. both my grandparents home _____

10. the Smiths car _____

11. Claude McKay poetry _____

12. the city mayor _____

13. many states governors _____

14. two schools principals _____

15. the navy flagship _____

16. any women organization _____

17. those stores managers _____

18. everybody ideas _____

19. my mother job _____

20. the Bradys vacation _____

21. someone viewpoint _____

22. the people choices _____

23. those firefighters bravery _____

24. Jorge newspapers _____

25. the earth surface _____

Copyright © by Holt, Rinehart and Winston. All rights reserved.

| LANGUAGE HANDBOOK | **15** | **PUNCTUATION** |

WORSHEET 2 | **Using Apostrophes (Rules 15 a, b)**

EXERCISE A   For each of the following sentences, underline the correct word in parentheses.

> **EXAMPLE 1.** May I borrow (*your*, *you're*) copy of Rachel Carson's *Silent Spring*?

1. (*Whose*, *Who's*) Siamese cat is that?

2. (*Your*, *You're*) right; Thor was the Norse god of storms and thunder.

3. Stop wiggling (*your*, *you're*) feet.

4. (*Their*, *They're*) rules for playing football are different from (*ours*, *our's*).

5. (*Its*, *It's*) time for your oboe lesson.

6. (*Their*, *They're*) sure that set of tools belongs to them.

7. (*Ours*, *Our's*) is a class full of hard workers.

8. (*Theirs*, *There's*) my grandmother's recipe for *fattoush*, a Syrian bread salad.

9. That is a picture of Raymond, (*whose*, *who's*) coming to visit us.

10. The beautiful macaw in the pet show is (*our's*, *ours*).

EXERCISE B   In the following sentences, each italicized word is followed by a line. If the word is correct, write *C* on the line. If it is incorrect, write the word correctly on the line.

> **EXAMPLE 1.** Bill said, "I think *it's* ____C____ *you're* ____your____ turn to clean the hamster's cage."

1. "*Don't* _____ tell me *its* _____ my turn again," Carla whined.

2. "*I'm* _____ sure *Ive* _____ done it two nights in a row.

3. *Have'nt* _____ I, Nora?"

4. *Noras'* _____ stamps held her interest, and she *did'nt* _____ answer *Carlas* _____ question.

5. She thought it was *Bill's* _____ problem.

6. "Oh, no," said Bill, "*youve* _____ skipped twice."

7. "*Someone's* _____ got to clean *it's* _____ cage, but I know it *isn't* _____ my turn."

8. "*Who's* _____ hamster is it—*yours* _____," Dad asked, "or *Carla's* _____ or *Noras* _____?"

9. "*It's* _____ *their's* _____ !" each shouted at once, pointing to the other two.

10. "Tonight," said Dad, "*its* _____ all of *yours* _____, and now *your* _____ all going to clean *its* _____ cage."

Copyright © by Holt, Rinehart and Winston. All rights reserved.

LANGUAGE
HANDBOOK **15** PUNCTUATION

| WORKSHEET 3 | Using Apostrophes (Rules 15 b, c)

EXERCISE A   Write the contraction of each of the following expressions.

EXAMPLE **1.** you have ___*you've*___

1. did not _____

2. I am _____

3. we will _____

4. who is _____

5. have not _____

6. we are _____

7. was not _____

8. 1999 _____

9. will not _____

10. there is _____

11. let us _____

12. you would _____

13. cannot _____

14. who will _____

15. here is _____

16. you are _____

17. Alonzo is _____

18. were not _____

19. they are _____

20. it is _____

EXERCISE B   On the line provided, write the plural of each of the following underlined expressions.

EXAMPLE **1.** too many *and*   ___*and's*___

1. three *7* _____

2. ± not *x* _____

3. friendly *hi* _____

4. *0* not *zeroes* _____

5. crossing your *t* _____

EXERCISE C   The following sentences contain both possessive nouns and contractions, but all the apostrophes are missing. Supply the necessary apostrophes.

EXAMPLE **1.** Who'll take Ambrose's place?

1. Mikis dog doesnt follow her to school anymore.

2. Lets not go bowling tonight.

3. Im happy about our new governors decision.

4. She hadnt heard about the teams victory.

5. Theyll use the students dining room.

Copyright © by Holt, Rinehart and Winston. All rights reserved.

Elements of Literature

WORSHEET 4 | Using Hyphens, Parentheses, and Dashes
(Rules 15 d–g)

EXERCISE A   On the line provided, show how each of the following words may be properly divided by using hyphens. If a word should not be divided, write "do not divide."

> EXAMPLE **1.** forlornly _____*for-lorn-ly*_____

1. alone _____

2. well-appointed _____

3. careful _____

4. togetherness _____

5. contraption _____

EXERCISE B   Most of the following sentences contain errors in the use of hyphens, parentheses, or dashes. Identify and correct each error. To remove incorrect punctuation, draw a delete mark (℘) through the error. To add punctuation, place a caret (∧) under the new punctuation mark and write the correct punctuation mark above it. If a sentence is correct, write *C* on the line provided.

> EXAMPLES _____ **1.** I'd love to stay for⁀yikes, it's late and I must go.
>
> _____ **2.** My aunt wants me to ba⁀
> (by-sit my little cousin.

_____ **1.** In parentheses at the end of the paragraph, a cross-reference directs the reader to page 234.

_____ **2.** Is seven-tenths of a cup more than three fourths of a cup?

_____ **3.** The surf shop is on Fifty seventh Street.

_____ **4.** In central Africa live peoples known as Pygmies, who here's a picture of them average between 4 feet and 4 feet 8 inches tall.

_____ **5.** Even today, many revere the words of the great Chinese philosopher Laotzu pronounced lou´dzu´.

_____ **6.** Only two thirds of the sheep have been sheared.

_____ **7.** The squirrels have scattered the nuts and the birdseed all over the ground.

_____ **8.** Reserved parking for persons with disabilities I can't believe people who do not have disabilities park in those spaces has helped many persons.

_____ **9.** My oldest brother will be twenty two in November.

_____ **10.** Shah Jahan 1592–1666 was the Indian emperor who built the Taj Mahal.

Continued ☞

Copyright © by Holt, Rinehart and Winston. All rights reserved.

Elements of Literature

_____ **11.** One quarter teaspoon of chili powder will not be enough.

_____ **12.** Attention, everyone; will everyone here please join us on this happy occasion.

_____ **13.** Mr.—oh, I've forgotten his name—left a message for you.

_____ **14.** When Israel fell to the Assyrians 722–721 B.C., many of Israel's tribes were scattered.

_____ **15.** The capital of Mozambique is Maputo pronounced mə poot´ō, which happens to be a seaport.

_____ **16.** Seventy three of the bolts of cloth must be delivered to 6789 East Thirty-second Street.

_____ **17.** Neither anthropologists nor linguists studying sites in Mexico completely understand Maya writings.

_____ **18.** I've been saving six months for that guitar in the window ooh, it's on sale.

_____ **19.** Bob Dylan born Robert Allen Zimmerman has contributed much to American music.

_____ **20.** Uncle Jim, do you know why we call these pretty wildflowers Dutchman's-breeches?

EXERCISE C   The following sentences contain errors in the use of hyphens, parentheses, and dashes. Identify and correct each error. To remove incorrect punctuation, draw a delete mark (⌿) through the error. To add punctuation, place a caret (∧) under the new punctuation mark and write the correct punctuation mark above it. If a sentence is correct, write *C* on the line provided.

EXAMPLE _____ **1.** Two-thirds of my guests each ate two and one half sandwiches.

_____ **1.** The Lewis and Clark expedition to the Northwest 1804–06 started and ended near St. Louis, Missouri.

_____ **2.** My grandmother, who is sixty five, goes to an aerobics class three times per week.

_____ **3.** The truth is and you may have suspected it already I never wanted to go to the dance.

_____ **4.** The banana muffin recipe called for one-half cup of canola oil, but all we had was olive oil.

_____ **5.** Joe went to the World Series game with his brother and his sister-in-law.

Copyright © by Holt, Rinehart and Winston. All rights reserved.

LANGUAGE HANDBOOK **15** **PUNCTUATION**

WORKSHEET 5 **Test (Rules 15 a–g)**

EXERCISE A   On the line provided, correctly write and punctuate each of the following word groups to show possession.

> **EXAMPLE 1.** the rajah family _____the rajah's family_____

1. the sun rays _____
2. the men hats _____
3. anyone promises _____
4. Romulus brother _____
5. Elisha Otis inventions _____

EXERCISE B   On the line provided, write the plural of each of the following underlined or italicized expressions.

> **EXAMPLE 1.** a word with four s ___s's___

1. counting to 100 by 5 _____
2. two u in "vacuum" _____
3. sentences with too many *so* _____
4. using & instead of *and* _____   _____
5. number with nine 0 _____

EXERCISE C   On the line provided, write the contraction of each of the following expressions.

> **EXAMPLE 1.** would not _____wouldn't_____

1. will not _____   6. it is _____
2. did not _____   7. has not _____
3. who is _____   8. here is _____
4. she will _____   9. could not _____
5. cannot _____   10. let us _____

Copyright © by Holt, Rinehart and Winston. All rights reserved.

Continued ☞

EXERCISE D   For each of the following sentences, underline the correct word in parentheses.

> **EXAMPLE 1.** (*Its, It's*) hind leg must be hurt.

1. (*Whose, Who's*) moccasins are these?

2. (*Your, You're*) essay shows a clear understanding of the Aztec culture.

3. (*Its, It's*) a pleasure to see you, Mr. Morales.

4. (*Your, You're*) reading Alberto Rios's book The Iguana Killer, aren't you?

5. (*Their, They're*) trip starts tomorrow, and (*their, they're*) going to Nova Scotia.

6. When will you write (*your, you're*) tribute to the Shawnee chief Tecumseh?

7. (*Ours, Our's*) is the first house on the left.

8. During (*their, they're*) vacation, (*their, they're*) leaving (*their, they're*) pet poodle in a kennel.

9. Their boat lost (*its, it's*) mast, but (*ours, our's*) is all right.

10. (*Whose, Who's*) going to repair (*yours, your's*) for you?

EXERCISE E   Each of the following sentences contains errors in the use of hyphens, parentheses, or dashes. On the line provided, rewrite each sentence, adding appropriate punctuation marks or taking out incorrect punctuation.

> **EXAMPLE 1.** The chef needs one and one half teaspoons of vanilla.
>
> *The chef needs one and one-half teaspoons of vanilla.*

1. Everyone in the family, the neighbors, and my friends love it when my little brother pretends to be a rock star.

_____

2. Now where did I put my here it is!

_____

3. Caracas is the capital of Venezuela see map on page 52.

_____

4. Look at the world map it's on page 37, and note the area covered by ice.

_____

5. Reserve half of these apples for applesauce; one half bushel will be plenty for making apple butter.

_____

Copyright © by Holt, Rinehart and Winston. All rights reserved.

WORKSHEET 1 Using Word Parts (Rules 16 a–c)

EXERCISE Divide each of the following words into parts (prefixes, roots, and suffixes). Then, write a definition based on the meanings of the parts. Check your definitions in a dictionary.

EXAMPLE **1.** teachable _teach|able—able to be instructed_ _____

1. hospitalize _____

_____

2. coauthor _____

_____

3. motivate _____

_____

4. transatlantic _____

_____

5. renewable _____

_____

6. oneness _____

_____

7. infirm _____

_____

8. revise _____

_____

9. antisocial _____

_____

10. goodness _____

_____

Copyright © by Holt, Rinehart and Winston. All rights reserved.

LANGUAGE HANDBOOK **16** SPELLING

| **WORKSHEET 2** | **Using Spelling Rules (Rules 16 d–f)** |

EXERCISE A   Fill in the blanks with the correct letters: *ie, ei, cede, ceed,* or *sede.*

EXAMPLE   **1.** n_*ei*_ghborhood

1. br_____f

2. w_____ght

3. y_____ld

4. ex_____

5. conc_____ve

6. sl_____gh

7. ch_____f

8. super_____

9. n_____ce

10. for_____gner

11. se_____

12. perc_____ve

13. fr_____nd

14. inter_____

15. h_____ght

16. pat_____nt

17. bel_____f

18. pre_____

19. n_____ther

20. p_____ce

EXERCISE B   Cross through the incorrect spellings of words containing *ie* or *ei* or ending in *-cede, -ceed,* or *-sede* in the following sentences. Then, write the correct spellings on the lines provided. If a sentence is correct, write *C.*

EXAMPLE   ___*exceeded*___   **1.** The size of the box ~~exceded~~ the shipping company's restrictions.

_____   **1.** "That costume is truly weird!" Dorothy exclaimed.

_____   **2.** James was voted "Most Likely to Succede."

_____   **3.** How long was the riegn of Ramses II in Egypt?

_____   **4.** The logger skillfully weilded the ax.

_____   **5.** Dave will start as a reciever for the football team.

_____   **6.** Computers superceded typewriters as well as calculators at Mom's office.

_____   **7.** The dinosaur bones were found in an ancient creek bed.

_____   **8.** Please procede to the next line.

_____   **9.** I believe in having a positive outlook, don't you?

_____   **10.** The frieght train passes here daily at 3:00 P.M.

Copyright © by Holt, Rinehart and Winston. All rights reserved.

Elements of Literature

LANGUAGE HANDBOOK 16 SPELLING

WORKSHEET 3 Adding Prefixes and Suffixes (Rules 16 g–m)

EXERCISE A On the line provided, spell each of the following words with the given prefix or suffix.

EXAMPLE **1.** mis + state = ___misstate___

1. brave + ly = _____
2. dry + ed = _____
3. nine + th = _____
4. right + ly = _____
5. knit + ing = _____
6. hope + ful = _____
7. fax + ed = _____
8. il + legal = _____
9. say + ing = _____
10. note + able = _____

11. preach + er = _____
12. mis + shape = _____
13. pay + ed = _____
14. embrace + able = _____
15. tow + ing = _____
16. quick + ly = _____
17. duty + ful = _____
18. dine + ing = _____
19. win + er = _____
20. clue + less = _____

EXERCISE B Cross through the incorrectly spelled words in the following sentences. Then, write the correct spellings on the lines provided. If a sentence is correct, write *C*.

EXAMPLE ___shining___ **1.** The sun is ~~shineing~~, and it's a beautiful day!

_____ **1.** The British sometimes refer to the radio as "the wireless."

_____ **2.** All three panellists were intelligent and quick.

_____ **3.** The large statues are very noticable.

_____ **4.** Ronald tryed to repair the air conditioner himself.

_____ **5.** Some nice person mowwed Mrs. Jackson's yard while she was away.

_____ **6.** I readly agree that you are correct.

_____ **7.** The disagreement made no sense to me or Lillian.

_____ **8.** "I don't approve of quiting a job half-done," Lynn said.

_____ **9.** The fuzzyness of those puppies is appealing.

_____ **10.** The baby cryed because it was hungry.

Copyright © by Holt, Rinehart and Winston. All rights reserved.

LANGUAGE HANDBOOK **16** SPELLING

| WORKSHEET 4 | **Forming Plurals of Nouns (Rules 16 n–y)**

EXERCISE A On the line provided, spell the plural form of each of the following nouns.

EXAMPLE **1.** Perez ___*Perezes*___

1. taboo _____
2. boy _____
3. treehouse _____
4. carpet _____
5. moose _____
6. soprano _____
7. wish _____
8. t _____
9. monkfish _____
10. box _____

11. 7 _____
12. McCoy _____
13. editor in chief _____
14. date _____
15. navy _____
16. two-year-old _____
17. Lee _____
18. goose _____
19. roof _____
20. cameo _____

EXERCISE B Cross through the incorrectly spelled words in the following sentences. Then, write the correct spellings on the lines provided. If a sentence is correct, write *C*.

EXAMPLE ___*soundtracks*___ **1.** Does she have the ~~soundtrack~~ of these movies?

_____ **1.** People were put in stockes as punishment in Colonial America.

_____ **2.** "The Sioux hunted on this land many years ago," the speaker said.

_____ **3.** Those two sister-in-laws are best friends and business partners.

_____ **4.** A construction crew dug four deep ditchs in our yard.

_____ **5.** Old sideswalk can be unsafe because they are cracked.

_____ **6.** The maple's leaves are bright orange and red in the fall.

_____ **7.** Our neighbors the Domingoes are not related to singer Plácido Domingo.

_____ **8.** "I want my dollys, please!" the child said.

_____ **9.** How many *4*'s are in your telephone number?

_____ **10.** These boxs are extremely heavy but must be moved.

Copyright © by Holt, Rinehart and Winston. All rights reserved.

WORKSHEET 5 Forming Plurals of Nouns (Rules 16 n–y)

EXERCISE A   On the line provided, spell the plural form of each of the following items.

EXAMPLE **1.** bird _____birds_____

1. tray _____

2. calf _____

3. piano _____

4. door prize _____

5. Jefferson _____

6. trout _____

7. bounty _____

8. thief _____

9. bench _____

10. *10* _____

11. mommy _____

12. shoehorn _____

13. pathway _____

14. potato _____

15. # _____

16. angle _____

17. lady-in-waiting _____

18. Kelly _____

19. mix _____

20. child _____

EXERCISE B   Cross through the incorrectly spelled words in the following sentences. Then, write the correct spellings on the lines provided. If a sentence is correct, write *C*.

EXAMPLE ____giraffes____ **1.** The ~~giraves~~ ate all the leaves from the trees.

_____ **1.** The Girls Scouts learned how to make flapjacks.

_____ **2.** The ambulance service operates in four countys.

_____ **3.** Do you always remember how many *ss* are in the word *necessary*?

_____ **4.** The city taxs go up only every other year.

_____ **5.** The Chinese boxes fascinated the youngsters.

_____ **6.** We have four different sizes of wrenchs.

_____ **7.** There are two wayes to safely exit the program.

_____ **8.** Both stereoes have high-quality sound.

_____ **9.** Remind the fours-year-old to finish their drawings in the morning.

_____ **10.** The Levys have been appointed to two steering committees.

Copyright © by Holt, Rinehart and Winston. All rights reserved.

LANGUAGE HANDBOOK 16 SPELLING

WORKSHEET 6 | Test (Rules 16 a–y)

EXERCISE A   Cross through the incorrectly spelled words in the following sentences. Then, write the correct spellings on the lines provided. If a sentence is correct, write *C*.

EXAMPLE ____*so's*____ **1.** Your letter contains too many ~~sos~~.

_____ **1.** The dangerous flood waters had reseded by morning.

_____ **2.** In the movie *Babe*, the sheeps are cooperative.

_____ **3.** There are five radios in our house now.

_____ **4.** Guess the wieght of a full-grown blue whale.

_____ **5.** I am studying the historys of the Aztec and the Maya peoples.

_____ **6.** "See you in the morning," Philip said sleepyly.

_____ **7.** My favorite blue shirt's came from thrift stores.

_____ **8.** Al's bating average is the highest on the team this year.

_____ **9.** Two twelve-year-olds stopped to admire the unique window display.

_____ **10.** "I hope I didn't misspeak," Darla said to the cousins.

EXERCISE B   The following paragraph contains twenty spelling errors. Cross through each error, and write the correct spelling above it.

             neighbors
EXAMPLE [1] Our ~~nieghbors~~, the Mercados, have many plants in their back yard.

[1] Growwing plants is one of their hobbys. [2] Their dayly routine includes diging and weeding. [3] The family is especially knowledgable about gardenes. [4] Anyone would conceed that their tomatos are prize worthy. [5] Fortunatly, they are very generous with thier harvest. [6] We look forward to recieving sweet corn and green beanes from them every summer. [7] Several familys who live nearby often find baskets of vegetables left on their patioes. [8] Sometimes, we have small partys to help the Mercados shell peas or pick strawberrys. [9] Mrs. Mercado's two sister-in-laws help her when she freezes boxs of fruits and vegetables for winter. [10] Mrs. Mercado uses those frozen foods to make delicious dishs for her family and freinds.

Continued ☞

Copyright © by Holt, Rinehart and Winston. All rights reserved.

Elements of Literature

EXERCISE C Cross through the incorrectly spelled words in the following sentences. Then, write the correct spellings on the lines provided. If a sentence is correct, write C.

EXAMPLE _____*stitches*_____ **1.** The ~~stitchs~~ in the needlework looked like tiny *x*'s.

_____ **1.** The Florezs attended parties the last two Fridays.

_____ **2.** "Are you doubtting my abilities?" Teresa asked.

_____ **3.** The sceintists are experts on geology and volcanoes.

_____ **4.** Does this shop sell stereos and televisions?

_____ **5.** The company is developing a videodisk on African American culture.

_____ **6.** Washing another's foots is an ancient custom.

_____ **7.** Both eyeswitness described the same series of events.

_____ **8.** "Prosede cautiously along the road, and watch for giraffes," the travel guide advised.

_____ **9.** Fred is an excellent painter, but painting is just one of his many hobbys.

_____ **10.** Snakes could overrun the island in a year.

EXERCISE D The following sentences contain ten spelling errors. Cross through each error, and write the correct spelling above it.

EXAMPLE **1.** Mexican Americans have ~~shurly~~ *surely* influenced American history.

1. Our class studied the heritage of Mexican Americans in Los Angeles.

2. Their achievments are impressive.

3. Mexican Americans helpped establish Los Angeles.

4. In fact, Los Angeles was just one of several important U.S. citys partly settled by Mexican Americans.

5. Mexican Americans also taught Western settlers about farming, mineing, and ranching.

6. In this book on Mexican American history, we saw beautyful pictures of a dance festival.

7. Hundredes of people participated in the festival.

8. Both mens and women wore colorful costumes.

9. The dances were as amazeing as the costumes.

10. I beleive the past and present are showcased at such festivals.

Copyright © by Holt, Rinehart and Winston. All rights reserved.

LANGUAGE HANDBOOK **17** GLOSSARY OF USAGE

| WORKSHEET 1 | Common Usage Problems

EXERCISE   Underline the word or expression in parentheses that is correct according to formal standard usage.

> **EXAMPLE 1.** We should fold the clothes (*as*, *like*) Mom instructed.

1. Would you please (*learn*, *teach*) me to make tortillas?

2. The golf course is a long (*way*, *ways*) from the clubhouse.

3. Angela is only five, but she reads really (*well*, *good*).

4. I (*could of*, *could have*) eaten all of the cantaloupe.

5. The jugglers have (*already*, *all ready*) performed.

6. The reason the raccoon came on the porch was (*that*, *because*) it was hungry.

7. Gerald does not want to go to camp (*without*, *unless*) I go too.

8. Doesn't that little house look protected (*between*, *among*) the two big oak trees?

9. (*Alot*, *A lot*) of people attended Erykah Badu's concert.

10. My mother rides her (*stationery*, *stationary*) bicycle every day.

11. Did Tom teach (*himself*, *hisself*) to play the harmonica?

12. There were (*fewer*, *less*) students at the game than we expected.

13. Mrs. Blackwood was (*some*, *somewhat*) disappointed in our test scores.

14. In basketball, dribbling is (*when a player moves the ball in short bounces, moving the ball in short bounces*).

15. "My car always runs (*bad*, *badly*) in cold weather," Jeremy said.

16. The principal spoke (*as if*, *like*) the rule would be changed.

17. I heard (*where*, *that*) the balloonists will try to set a new flight record.

18. Please hand me (*them*, *those*) glasses, Jenny.

19. People (*everywheres*, *everywhere*) enjoy stories about tricksters.

20. Did you (*choose*, *chose*) the movie we're seeing tonight?

21. Craig (*hadn't ought*, *ought not*) to have stayed up so late.

22. Did you hear the comedian (*who*, *which*) warmed up the audience?

23. (*How come you didn't*, *Why didn't you*) finish your breakfast?

24. We were (*sort of*, *somewhat*) reassured by Ms. Lee's words.

25. (*My cousins they*, *My cousins*) live in Orlando, Florida.

Copyright © by Holt, Rinehart and Winston. All rights reserved.

Elements of Literature

| **WORKSHEET 2** | **Common Usage Problems** |

EXERCISE A   Underline the word or expression in parentheses that is correct according to formal standard usage.

> **EXAMPLE 1.** Here is some blue (<u>*stationery*</u>, *stationary*) for your letters.

1. It's (*all right, alright*) with me to leave tomorrow instead of today.

2. Wole Soyinka is the person (*which, who*) won the Nobel Prize in literature in 1986.

3. "Don't jump (*off, off of*) that table, Elly!" Dad yelled.

4. Someone (*had ought, ought*) to fix the broken window.

5. Do you know (*why, how come*) the sky is blue?

6. (*Like, As*) people say, don't borrow trouble.

7. Bonnie Sue was (*rather, kind of*) surprised by the news.

8. The (*horses, horses they*) ran through the gate and beyond the windmill.

9. (*Among, Between*) the five of us, we have all the tools for the project.

10. "That is (*real, extremely*) nice of you to offer to help," Ms. Serling said.

EXERCISE B   Most of the following sentences contain errors in usage. If a sentence contains an error, cross out the error and write the correct word on the line provided. If a sentence is correct, write *C*.

> **EXAMPLE** ___*chose*___ **1.** Allen ~~choose~~ not to compete this year.

_____ **1.** Our team performed good during the Quiz Bowl.

_____ **2.** Do you know where the Taj Mahal is?

_____ **3.** A neighbor is learning me to sew Hawaiian quilts.

_____ **4.** What would happen if the piñata busted open?

_____ **5.** Dinner should be already by the time we get home.

_____ **6.** I read that the Java is a breed of domestic chicken.

_____ **7.** Rick has less breaks at his new job, but he likes the work.

_____ **8.** Sheila must of called while I was at the library.

_____ **9.** I feel bad that you lost the election.

_____ **10.** My missing sock is somewheres in the house.

Copyright © by Holt, Rinehart and Winston. All rights reserved.

LANGUAGE HANDBOOK **17** **GLOSSARY OF USAGE**

| WORKSHEET 3 | Test

EXERCISE A In the following sentences, underline the word or expression in parentheses that is correct according to formal standard usage.

> **EXAMPLE 1.** The weather has cleared (*some, somewhat*) since noon.

1. I (*should have, should of*) brought my headphones for the car trip.

2. Remarkably, the man remained absolutely (*stationery, stationary*) for eight hours.

3. Tamara is (*teaching, learning*) me a native dance of Bali.

4. All three friends reacted (*bad, badly*) to the unexpected news.

5. We would have to drive a long (*way, ways*) to reach the Pacific Ocean.

6. The choice is (*between, among*) a station wagon and a sport-utility vehicle.

7. Can you tell me (*how come, why*) Jorge Ulica wrote "An Extraordinary Touchdown"?

8. Aaron (*hisself, himself*) told us about entering the hog-calling contest.

9. "The chickens always lay (*less, fewer*) eggs in the winter," Anne said.

10. Here is the mask (*who, that*) frightened my baby sister.

EXERCISE B Most of the following sentences contain errors in usage. If a sentence contains an error, cross out the error and write the correction on the line provided. If a sentence is correct, write *C*.

> **EXAMPLE** ____all right____ **1.** I did ~~alright~~ on the test after all.

_____ 1. The reason the picture looks strange is because it is upside down.

_____ 2. You can't leave without I give my permission.

_____ 3. Colette she is a successful public relations executive.

_____ 4. Have you already told Mrs. Ling about the accident?

_____ 5. She is a person which likes to swim every day.

_____ 6. You acted like you'd never heard of tamales.

_____ 7. Samuel hadn't ought to have mentioned the problem to you.

_____ 8. I have a flashlight, but I don't know where it is at.

_____ 9. The Olympic skater from Russia skated good.

_____ 10. The carpenters busted the picture window when they were hammering.

Copyright © by Holt, Rinehart and Winston. All rights reserved.

Continued ☞

Elements of Literature

EXERCISE C   In the following sentences, underline the word or expression in parentheses that is correct according to formal standard usage.

>   **EXAMPLE 1.** The young boy screamed when the balloon (*burst*, *busted*).

1. Black ink looks best on this gold (*stationery, stationary*).

2. I read (*where, that*) the Shoshones lived in Idaho.

3. The owners must be out to lunch, (*like, as*) the sign indicates.

4. "The new roller coaster is probably (*alot, a lot*) of fun," Chen said.

5. The play (*could of, could have*) been better with more rehearsal.

6. We've been (*everywheres, everywhere*) in the neighborhood looking for our missing cat.

7. In baseball, a foul ball is (*when a player hits the ball, a ball hit*) outside foul lines.

8. The student (*chose, choose*) to give a report on African American folk tales.

9. Lu sat down because she wasn't feeling (*good, well*).

10. The editors were (*kind of, rather*) surprised by the results of the opinion poll.

EXERCISE D   Most of the following sentences contain errors in formal standard usage. If a sentence contains an error, cross out the error and write the correction on the line provided. If a sentence is correct, write *C*.

>   **EXAMPLE** _parents want_   **1.** The ~~parents they want~~ to vote on the issue of year-round school.

_____ **1.** Wait for me outside of the Alamo entrance, please.

_____ **2.** "I want someone to learn me to drive," Fay said.

_____ **3.** The handball game jai alai is real popular in Latin America.

_____ **4.** There was concern between the student body after the board's decision.

_____ **5.** We will proceed as though we know what we're doing.

_____ **6.** Hiking the Appalachian Trail sounds sort of challenging.

_____ **7.** "The orange looks okay, but it tastes badly," Ruth Ann said.

_____ **8.** Let me hear them jazz recordings of Dizzy Gillespie.

_____ **9.** The girls were all ready for the concert an hour early.

_____ **10.** Are there less lemons in this bag?

Copyright © by Holt, Rinehart and Winston. All rights reserved.